SATURDAY NIGHT, FULL MOON

Saturday Night, FULL MOON

Intriguing Stories of Kabbalah Sages,
Chasidic Masters,
and other Jewish Heroes

volume 1

By

YERACHMIEL MICHAEL TILLES

MENORAH BOOKS

HONG KONG · JERUSALEM · LAS VEGAS

Saturday Night, FULL MOON

Intriguing Stories of Kabbalah Sages,
Chasidic Masters, and other Jewish Heroes

VOLUME I

Published by MENORAH BOOKS

EDITING: Chaim Natan Firszt, Ashirah Yosefah

COVER DESIGN: Gal Narunsky

TYPOGRAPHY & LAYOUT: Gal Narunsky

PRINTER: Old City Press, Jerusalem

Information and inquiries: administrator@menorah-books.com

ISBN: 978-1-940516-07-3

Volume One: First Edition

FOR ORDERS:

INTERNET: www.menorah-books.com

EMAIL: orders@menorah-books.com

Dedicated

*To all those who over the last fifteen years
encouraged me to produce this book:
readers and live audiences; students, colleagues
and Shabbat guests; friends and relatives,
especially my wife, the foundation of our
marriage, our family, our home.*

אשת חיל מי ימצא ... ואת עלית על כולנה.

Dedicated by the

Bendahan Family:

Albert and Leslie and all the children.

With special blessings to

Alegria Bendahan

for good health and long life

And for the soul elevations of

Shmuel ben Amram Bendahan

and

Yitzchak ben Baruch Stefanski

Rabbi Shneur Zalman of Liadi,
the first Chabad Rebbe, stated:

"To us, his senior disciples, a teaching of the Maggid of Mezeritch was [part of] the Oral Torah. But when the Maggid told us a story, it was the Written Torah itself."

—

"Telling stories of the tzadikim draws down the light of the Moshiach into this world and expels much darkness and many troubles from the world."

Rebbe Nachman of Bratzlav

Table of Contents

PART THREE

Chasidic Masters: the 2nd hundred years
1820–1920 (C.E.)

Foreword

What a happy occasion! The first book of stories from Ascent. The Ascent Center in Safed is a place where thousands of people come annually to find out more about what it means to be Jewish. Perhaps the most successful vehicle to do this is through the stories about tzadikim, mystics, sages, chasidim and men and women of action. The tales of the righteous are not simply historical records of events that happened many years ago, rather each story serves as an example of how we can better live our lives with integrity.

Each expert story teller recounts his stories through his or her own particular lens, with his or her unique style. Stories have been a part of the Ascent tradition for 30 years and Rabbi Tilles, one of Ascent's founders, is our master story teller. After decades of sharing his wealth of knowledge, we bless him in this most successful endeavor and pray that this book is not only well received, but that it is the first of many to come.

Rabbi Shaul Leiter
Director, Ascent of Safed

Approbation

The stories of Rabbi Tilles are tremendously creative and engaging. Rabbi Tilles enables the reader to enter the life of the story — to experience in a very real and tangible way its feelings, beauty, life and drama. Rabbi Tilles' stories have been on the front page of the Living Jewish weekly publication for years. People will approach me on the street, in shops, and enthusiastically tell me how much they enjoyed a particular story. The Living Jewish readership is particularly diverse yet the stories have the ability to appeal to people from a wide array of backgrounds. Rabbi Tilles has an amazing gift and I am very excited that with this new book more people will have the opportunity to enjoy and benefit from his stories.

Aaron Schmidt

Editor, Living Jewish

Introduction

This is an introduction, so let me introduce myself to those of you who don't know me already.

I have been hearing, reading and telling Jewish-Chasidic stories for 40 years — including 35 years here in Tzefat (Safed) — and translating, adapting, editing, compiling, and e-mailing one per week for the past sixteen years to many thousands of subscribers and readers. Now many of them have been translated into numerous languages as well.

From my archives, I culled about a hundred stories which I feel are book worthy, and reasonably trustworthy; with verifiable details or at least from reliable sources, yet are mostly not so well known that you would have read them in other collections. This is enough for three volumes, as I lean toward longer stories. The first and third volumes are general; the second, due to appear a year after this one, G-d willing, will focus on the cycle of Jewish holidays.

In this first volume, the stories are divided into four distinct time periods, in approximate chronological order within each section. However, there is no need whatsoever to read this book in page order, I've included in the Table of Contents a few intriguing sentences about each story so that you can easily envision what you are getting into.

In addition, each story is introduced with some biographical background about the main characters. Also, for those of you who feel the need, I provide suggestions about how to connect each story to specific times in the Jewish year and to certain main themes. This information is also available in the indexes.

At the end of each story I credit my source/sources. I also cite where each story was first published, even though many of them have been extensively revised over the years and while preparing this book.

I could now launch into a pithy discourse about the significance of Saturday nights in Judaism, with an emphasis on storytelling, but why should I keep you from the stories themselves. Instead, I relegated it to the back of the book, as an appendix.

Also saved for the back is a full page of acknowledgements, to thank the wonderful people that have helped me to get this book out. The book itself is long overdue, so I won't keep you any longer. Enjoy!

Yerachmiel Tilles

In the Mystical City of Tzefat (Safed) in the Holy Land of Israel
Erev Shabbat, Yud-Tet Kislev 5774 (November 22, 2013 C.E.)

Email: **YTilles3@gmail.com**
To receive a new story weekly by email, free, write to:
weekly@AscentOfSafed.com *(story)*

Preface

A Note on Some Confusing Terms and Spellings

I tried hard to sweep the manuscript free of Hebrew words and idioms, assuming only that the reader would be familiar with the names of the Jewish holidays, and that he or she would appreciate having the month-names of the Jewish calendar (Jewish years have been given their Gregorian calendar equivalents, and vice versa, but the two systems of months are not parallel). The few words that may have been missed by my broom are (hopefully) parenthetically translated; so there is no need for the customary glossary one might find in a book such as this.

This "glossary" is different, as the title clearly indicates. Furthermore, it contains only five entries. All but the fourth are in modern English dictionaries, but in usage the meanings of the first three tend to slide around according to context, and their spellings vary, especially the fifth and last.

1. Chasid   2. Rebbe   3. Tzadik   4. Z'l, etc.   5. Safed

1. Chasid *(Variant spellings: Chassid, Hassid)***.** Each of these three can also be spelled with a lower case 'c'. To form the plural put "im" at the end, chasidim. The adjective is chasidic. The movement and also its philosophy-theology are called 'chasidut' in Hebrew, 'chasidus' in Eastern European dialect, and 'chasidism' in academic English. Each of these may be properly spelled with a single or double 's'. My personal preference is lower case and one 's' as is used throughout this book.

Although the word "chasid" has distinctly different connotations depending on where one is on the Jewish spectrum, in common *chasidic* usage, and in this book, 'chasid' denotes a Jew who is devotedly attached to a chasidic *rebbe* (see next term). It must be conceded though, that the absoluteness of this usage was weakened in the generation after WWII, as a result of the cursed Nazis murdering as many rebbes as they could capture and identify.

2. Rebbe. Grammatically, "rebbe" is the first person possessive form of "rabbi". Thus, "rebbe" means my rabbi/teacher. In chasidic terminology, "Rebbe" (note the capital 'R') denotes a spiritual master and mentor with acute spiritual insight, nearly all of whom can trace genealogical or teacher-student descent from the Baal Shem Tov, the Maggid of Mezritch (his successor), or one of the Maggid's inner circle of disciples (many of whom, but obviously not all, can be found in the stories in Section A of this book).

To complicate it even further, 'Rav', 'Reb', 'R.' may also show up a few times. A *Rav* is a higher level than a *Rabbi*, qualified to make decisions in many more areas of Jewish law. *Reb* is akin to Mr., and 'R.' can stand for Rav, Rabbi or Reb, depending on the context.

3. Tzadik. (Plural: tzadikim; variant spelling: tzaddik, tzaddikim). Tzadik can mean a righteous person, or even more, a (nearly) perfectly pure and righteous person. In this book, the word denotes the latter.

(The colloquial usage of this word is often more familiar, where it is often used to describe someone who does a lot of good deeds, which in quantity or quality outweigh his bad ones. For example, Rosh Hashana (The Jewish New Year), we bless each other to be inscribed in the Book of the Righteous). Tzadik can also be used to refer to someone declared innocent or righteous by a court, whether Heavenly or earthly.)

To put 2 and 3 together, every Rebbe is supposedly a tzadik, at least at some level, but not every tzadik has to be a Rebbe, or even chasidic.

4. *Z'l, etc.* *Z'l, ztz'l* and *a'h* are abbreviations for the Hebrew expressions *zichrono l'bracha, zichron tzadik l'bracha*, and *alav hashalom*. These are expressions of respect for the departed which mean (respectively), 'may his memory be for a blessing', 'may the memory of this righteous one be for a blessing', and 'may he rest in peace' (literally, 'May peace be upon him'). In English, z'L and a'h are commonly abbreviated ob'm ("of blessed memory"), and r.i.p. ("rest in peace"). In this book, for the sake of the flow of the English, I have dispensed with all of these Hebrew expressions and their abbreviations.

5. *Safed.* The "City of Kabbalah", the "Capital of the Upper Galilee", a site that is mentioned in many of these stories. It is also the town I reside in. There are easily over a dozen different spellings extant. The entry spelling 'Safed' (emphasis on the first syllable) is the best known and comes from the Arab/British name for our fair city. I prefer not to use it, as its connotation is quite different than the Hebrew original. The Israeli government uses 'Zefat' on highway signs. Maps in English for tourists usually have 'Safed'. Closest to the actual Hebrew pronunciation (of *tsadi-fei-tof*) is probably 'Ts'fat'(emphasis on the last syllable). Unlike the above four entries, I haven't made up my mind firmly on this one yet. Among the English spelling residents of our special town, it remains a unresolved topic. I decided to use 'Tzefat' in this book for a reason that I no longer remember!

A NOTE ON HEBREW WORDS AND IDIOMS

This book is a collection of stories; each story fully able to rest on its own merits. As such, the standard grammatical practice of *italicizing* the first appearance of a word of a foreign language (in this case Hebrew) and thereafter using it in standard font, has been expanded and adapted somewhat. The first time a Hebrew word or idiom is used in the book, it will be placed in *italics* (with an English explanation following in parentheses). Thereafter, the first time such words appear in individual stories, they will also be italicized, and if deemed appropriate, explained again in parentheses. An exception to this rule will be in the case of frequently used and commonly understood Hebrew proper names and titles, Hebrew expressions and variations on words such as *Torah, Talmud, Kabbalah, kosher,* etc., as well as the examples cited above in the Preface.

PART ONE

Kabbalists of 16th–17th Century (C. E.) Tzefat and Jerusalem

1 Revealed on a Forehead

16th Century
(middle)
Tzefat

Biographical notes for this story:

Rabbi **Yitzchak Luria** — the Holy ***Ari*** [of blessed memory: 5294– 5 Av 5332 (1534–1572 C.E.)], the leader of the **Tzefat** kabbalists during the last years of his life, was the most influential Jewish mystic since Rabbi **Shimon Bar Yochai** 1,400 years earlier. Much of chasidic thought is based on the Ari's teachings, as recorded by his main disciple, Rabbi **Chaim Vital**.

Rabbi **Moshe (ben Mordechai) Galante** [of blessed memory: 5300–5374 (1540–1614 C.E.)] was one of four Tzefat rabbis (along with Rabbi Yosef Caro, author of *Shulchan Aruch*) to receive rabbinical ordination from Rabbi Yaakov Beirav in the 'renewal of biblical-level *semicha*' (rabbinical ordination) controversy. He and his older brother, Rabbi **Avraham Galante** (1540–1588), who subsequently became the city's chief rabbi, lived in Tzefat in the 1500's.

This story can be related to:

Weekly Readings: *Ki Teitze* — Deuteronomy 24:14–15 ("Do not withhold the wages due to your poor or destitute hired hand ... You must give him his wage on the day that it is due.")

Jewish Calendar Date: *Menachem Av* 5 (4 days before *Tisha B'Av*) — *yahrzeit* of the Holy Ari

Main Themes: Honesty in business, Practical kabbalah

Other Topics: Tzefat , Belief in tzadikim, Divine inspiration, Humility, Galante

Revealed on a Forehead

THE PIOUS AND WELL-KNOWN scholar, Rabbi ***Moshe Galante*** of Tzefat (Safed), heard an account from his brother about the extraordinary holiness of Rabbi ***Yitzchak Luria*** (the Ari), the foremost Kabbalist of the generation. He decided to seek his advice. Perhaps the Ari could help him to further perfect himself, he thought excitedly.

"Frankly, I never thought before that you were anyone special, but now that I have heard differently, I have come to request of you a *tikun* [rectification] for my soul."

"Why ask me?" asked the Ari, modestly, "I am not a prophet." After several further rounds of request and denial, R. Galante pleaded, "It is stated that you have the power to discern the root of a person's soul and his previous incarnations, but I am not asking for that. I just want to know what have I done that requires rectification from the day my soul was born into this body until now, so that I will not have to undergo any further reincarnations. I know you can see such things on a person's forehead. Please read mine!"

At this impassioned plea, the Ari gazed intently at R. Moshe for a moment and murmured, "Borderline theft."

Instantly, R. Galante jumped up and ran off, not even saying goodbye. As soon as he reached his home, he stripped off his clothes and donned sackcloth and ashes. Throwing himself to the ground, he cried out to G-d, weeping and slapping himself the entire time. Finally, he sent for all the employees of his textile business and demanded that if anyone felt that he or she had been shortchanged or paid unfairly in any way, to please present a claim *right then*, even for the tiniest amount. When they all denied any wrongdoing on his part, R. Galante exclaimed; "What are you doing to me! Don't you see what condition I am in? The Ari has said that I am guilty of borderline theft."

He then spread out a large amount of money before them and said: "Each of you take however much you wish. If I owe you anything, then the debt is cancelled; if not, it is a present." Even then no one responded, until finally one woman stepped forward and took a small sum.

R. Galante then hurried back to the Ari, who assured him that his forehead no longer revealed any trace of sin. He went on to explain that the woman who had taken the money did a delicate kind of weaving, and it could be considered that she deserved a slightly higher wage than the other workers.

Needless to say, after this episode, R. Galante always acted towards the Ari with the greatest of respect.

Source: Translated and freely adapted by Yerachmiel Tilles from the Hebrew weekly *Sichat HaShavua*, #721. (First published *Shivchei HaAri*. (First published in *Ascent Quarterly* #16 — also printed in *Kfar Chabad* #770.)

In Defense of Elijah 2

16th Century (2nd half) Tzefat

Biographical notes for this story:

Rabbi **Moshe Al-Sheich** [of blessed memory: 5268– 13 Nissan 5353 (1508– April 1593 C.E.)]was the author of many works, including important analytical explanations of Scriptures, which are highly regarded, and some of which are now available in English. He was a senior student of Rabbi Yosef Caro and a member of his Rabbinical Court.

This story can be related to:

Weekly Readings: *Vayera* — Genesis 18:1–8 (See Rashi: From verse 3 we derive that "Greater is caring for guests than communing with G-d in a state of prophecy")

Jewish Calendar Date: *Nissan* 13 (2 days before Passover) — yahrzeit of the Alsheich

Main Themes: Saturday night, Elijah the Prophet

Other Topics: Wives, Wealth and poverty, Hospitality, Tzefat

In Defense of Elijah

RABBI MOSHE ALSHEICH was the head of a large yeshiva in 16th Century *Tzefat* (Safed). He had received rabbinical ordination from Rabbi Yosef Caro, author of *Shulchan Aruch* [Code of Jewish Law]. He was a wealthy and extremely charitable man, in addition to being a great Torah scholar. One Saturday night after Shabbat departed, as he was passing by the home of a certain poor man, he heard the man joyfully wish his wife a good week, and begin to sing the hymn Eliyahu HaNavi [Elijah the Prophet]. His wife, however, interrupted bitterly, "What are you so happy about? You know that the children have been hungry for many days and there is still no food in the house and no firewood either. So where is Eliyahu HaNavi in whose honor you sing?"

Upon his return home, R. Alsheich filled a sack with gold coins. He then covered his face and quietly retraced his steps, opened the door of the couple's house, and threw in the sack of money and ran off.

This anonymous generosity raised a great stir in Heaven. However, the heavenly prosecuting angel said that it was nothing extraordinary, and that R. Alsheich should not be specially rewarded until he himself goes down to test him.

The next Shabbat, a poor man suddenly appeared in the synagogue and announced, "I am hungry! Who will feed me?" R. Alsheich immediately invited him for the Shabbat meal. The man devoured all the food that was set in front of him and then cried out that he was still hungry. Further helpings also failed to satisfy him. R. Alsheich was so concerned that he served the man all the food that had been prepared for himself and his family for the entire Shabbat. The guest ate everything up at once and again cried out that he was still hungry. R. Alsheich then ran over to some neighbors and took whatever food they could give him, but it was not enough to satisfy his ravenous guest.

So it continued all through the Shabbat. The poor man gluttonously consumed whatever he was given and then cried out that he was still hungry. In the end R. Alsheich said to him, "Today is Shabbat and there is nothing more I can do, but with G-d's help, after Shabbat I shall try to feed you until you are satisfied."

After Shabbat, he sent an ox to be slaughtered, but afterwards it was found to be *treif* [ritually unfit], and another ox had to be brought. This one also turned out to be unfit.

All told, thirty-nine oxen were slaughtered and all were found to be treif! This caused R. Alsheich great financial loss, but he kept insisting that he had to satisfy the hungry man. Finally, the fortieth ox was declared to be *kosher* (fit according to Jewish law), but before they could prepare it, the poor man disappeared.

This extraordinary demonstration of kindness caused another great commotion in the heavenly court. A decree was issued that one of the seventy faces of the Torah should be revealed to R. Alsheich, and an angel was immediately dispatched to impart the knowledge to him.

At his time, Rabbi Yosef Caro was the Chief Rabbi of Tzefat. He arrived at the synagogue the following Shabbat as the service was about to begin, but when he looked up at R. Alsheich's seat and saw that it was empty he ordered the congregation to wait, for it had been revealed to him that Rabbi Alsheich had become very great in Torah. When it was time for the weekly discourse about the Reading of the Law which R. Yosef Caro always gave, he asked R. Alsheich to ascend to the pulpit and speak in his place. R. Alsheich refused at first, insisting he wasn't capable. Only when R. Yosef Caro finally ordered him to speak did he agree. R. Alsheich ascended the platform and delivered a discourse. Everyone was amazed by his profundity.

From that day on, the Alsheich *HaKodesh* (the Holy Alsheich, as he came to be called) delivered the weekly address each Shabbat. He also began to write down his highly regarded explanations on most of the 24 books of the Torah.

Source: Adapted by Yerachmiel Tilles from several written and oral sources. (First published in *Ascent Quarterly* #18 — also printed in *Kfar Chabad* #769.)

A Delicious Offering 3

16th Century
(2nd half)
Tzefat

Biographical notes for this story:

Rabbi **Yitzchak Luria** — the Holy ***Ari*** [of blessed memory: 5294– 5 Av 5332 (1534–1572 C.E.)], was the leader of the Tzefat Kabbalists and during the last years of his life was the most influential Jewish mystic since Rabbi Shimon Bar Yochai, who lived 1,600 years before. Much of chasidic thought is based on the Ari's teachings, as recorded by his main disciple, Rabbi Chaim Vital.

This story can be related to:

Weekly Readings: *Emor* — Leviticus 24:5–9 (the twelve loaves of showbread)

Jewish Calendar Date: 5th of *Av* (4 days before Tisha B'Av) — *yahrzeit* of the Holy Ari

Main Themes: Conversos, Shabbat

Other Topics: Tzefat, Holy Temple, Innocence, Faith, Wives, Torah study

A Delicious Offering

In the mid sixteenth century, a *Converso** (forced convert) Jew from Portugal moved to the holy city of Tzefat (Safed). Deprived of the opportunity to do so in his youth, he was overjoyed to finally be able to practice the religion of his ancestors openly.

Years later, he heard a talk by the rabbi of the synagogue about *lechem hapanim*, the showbread [see Leviticus 24:5–9], which was offered in the Holy Temple each Friday before Shabbat, and miraculously remained fresh until the following Friday seven days later. After explaining the various laws and procedures governing this offering and touching on its mystical significance, the rabbi sighed deeply and bemoaned that, because of our sins, we no longer had this ready means to propitiate Gd.

The Jew took these words to heart. When he arrived home, he asked his wife to prepare two special challahs on Friday. He related to her all the details he remembered from the lecture on showbread. She should sift the flour thirteen times, knead it while she was in a state of purity, and bake the dough very well in their oven. He told her that he wished to present these loaves as an offering to G-d. Hopefully, He would consider them an acceptable sacrifice, and eat them.

His wife loyally fulfilled his request, and early that Friday afternoon, when no one was likely to be in the shul, the man brought the loaves there under his cloak. He prayed and cried that G-d should look upon his offering with favor, and eat and enjoy the lovely, freshly baked bread. He went on and on, like an errant son begging his father for forgiveness. Then he placed the loaves, wrapped, in the Holy Ark, beneath the Torah scrolls, and quickly left for home.

The *shammash* (caretaker) of the shul arrived later that day to complete the preparations of the shul for the holy Shabbat. One of his duties was to check that the Torah scroll was rolled to the proper place for the reading the next morning. When he opened the Ark, he was surprised to see a package had been neatly placed inside. He opened it, and there were two fine-looking challah loaves! He had no idea where they had come from, but he didn't think too much about it. He simply decided to take them home and eat them. After all, they looked and smelled delicious!

And they were delicious. The caretaker was delighted with this unexpected fringe benefit of his job.

That evening, the excited Jew waited impatiently for the end of the prayers. When everyone had left the shul, he approached the Ark in great trepidation, and swung open its doors. The loaves were not there! He was so happy. He hurried home to share his joy with his wife. He innocently proclaimed G-d had not disdained the poor efforts of such insignificant people as themselves. Indeed, He had accepted their two loaves, and eaten them while they were still warm!

"Therefore", he exhorted her, "let us not be lazy, for we have no other way to honor Him, and we see that He loves our bread. Every week we must try to give Him this pleasure, with the same care and devotion that we did this first time."

His wife was swayed by his wholehearted excitement, and gladly cooperated. Every Friday morning she faithfully prepared two beautiful loaves, paying careful attention to every detail, great and small, and every Friday afternoon he delivered them to the shul, and earnestly prayed and pleaded with God for their acceptance.

Every Friday the caretaker would come along, take the loaves, and happily eat the delicious challahs, and every Friday night the Jew from Portugal ecstatically informed his wife that once again their meager offering had been accepted.

So it went, week after week, for months.

One Friday, the rabbi of the shul stayed much later than usual, until the afternoon. It was the same rabbi who had given the speech about "showbread" that had so inspired the Converso from Portugal. He was standing on the *bima* [reading platform], reviewing the sermon he planned to give the next day, when, to his surprise, he saw one of his congregants enter carrying two loaves of bread, walk up to the Ark, and deposit them inside. He realized that the man was unaware of his presence, and he heard him utter fervent prayers for G-d to accept his offering and enjoy the challahs.

The rabbi listened in astonishment. At first he was silent, but as he began to understand what was going on, his anger rose. Finally he was unable to restrain himself any longer, and burst out in fury, "Stop! You fool! How can you think that our G-d eats and drinks? It is a terrible sin to ascribe human or any physical qualities to G-d Al-mighty. You actually believe it is the L-rd who takes your measly loaves? Why, it is probably the shammash who eats them."

At that moment the caretaker entered the shul, blithely expecting to pick up his challahs, as usual. He was a bit startled to see the rabbi and another man standing there. The rabbi immediately confronted him, "Tell this man why you came here now, and who has been taking the two challahs he has been bringing each week."

The caretaker freely admitted it. He wasn't embarrassed at all. He couldn't understand why the rabbi was so agitated, and why he was yelling at the other man who looked so unhappy, whom he knew to be an unlearned but sincere Jew.

As the rabbi continued his rebuke, the man burst into tears. He was crushed. Not only had he not done a mitzvah as he had thought, it seemed he was guilty of a great sin. He apologized to the rabbi for having misunderstood his lesson about the showbread, and begged him to forgive him. He left the shul in shame and despair. How could he have been so wrong? What was he to do now?

Shortly thereafter, a messenger from the Holy Ari [**Rabbi Yitzchak Luria**] strode into the shul and approached the rabbi. In the name of his master, he told the rabbi to go home, say goodbye to his family, and prepare himself, because by the designated time for his sermon the next morning, his soul will already have departed to its eternal rest. Thus it had been announced from Heaven.

The rabbi couldn't believe what he had just heard, nor could the disciple explain it to him. So the rabbi went directly to the Ari, who confirmed the message and added, as gently as possible, "I heard that it is because you halted G-d's pleasure, the likes of which He hasn't enjoyed since the day the Holy Temple was destroyed. That is what He felt when this innocent uneducated Jew would bring his two precious loaves to your shul each week, faithfully offering them to G-d from the depths of his heart with joy and awe, and believing that G-d had taken them, until you irrevocably destroyed his innocence. For this the decree was sealed against you, and there is no possibility to change it."

The rabbi went home and sadly told his family all that had transpired. By the time of the sermon the next morning, his soul had already departed** to hear Torah in the Heavenly Academy, exactly as the *Ari* had said.

Source: Translated-supplemented by Yerachmiel Tilles from *Kfar Chabad Magazine* #885, based on *Mishnat Hachamim*, whose author, Rabbi Moshe Hagiz (1572–?), writes that he heard this story from reliable people in Tzefat who were there when it happened. (First published on *AscentOf Safed com.*)]

Translator's notes:

—

* Jews that went through the motions of conversion in order to avoid expulsion or execution by the Inquisition. Let's avoid the more common term, *Marrano,* which is a highly insulting term.

** A tradition in *Tzefat* has it that the rabbi until this point was living 'extra' years, beyond his original allotment, in the merit of the pleasure he indirectly caused G-d, through his lecture on the showbread.

The Umbrella Parade

Biographical notes for this story:

Rabbi **Moshe (ben Yonatan) Galante** [of blessed memory: ?–5449 (?–1689 C.E.)], was the grandson of Rabbi Moshe ben Mordechai Galante (see story #1 in this book). He moved from Tzefat to Jerusalem around the year 5415 (1655 C.E.), where he became the Chief Rabbi of the city and was known as *Rav HaMagen*. He also founded a large yeshiva there, and was succeeded as its head by his main student, the great rabbinical authority known as the "*Pri Chadash*."

This story can be related to:

Weekly Readings: *Vayera* — Genesis 18:1–8 (See Rashi: from verse 3 we derive that caring for guests is greater than communing with G-d in a state of prophecy)

Jewish Calendar Date: *Nissan* 13 (2 days before Passover) — yahrzeit of the Alsheich

Main Themes: Saturday night, Elijah the Prophet

Other Topics: Wives, Wealth and poverty, Hospitality, Tzefat

The Umbrella Parade

Centuries ago, before the days of water pipes and irrigation, the residents of Jerusalem were dependent for all their water needs on the large cisterns they had dug out and lined. Each year the winter rains would fill the cisterns, and the people would draw water from them the entire year.

Once, in the early decades of the 5400's (mid 17th Century C.E.), there was a serious drought. One by one the winter months came and went, yet the skies remained as clear and pure blue as on a pleasant summer day. The earth was dry and cracked in the unyielding gardens and fields, and the water level of the cisterns was dropping at an alarming rate.

More days passed. Already the winter season was drawing to an end, but still, no rain. Even the elders of the city couldn't recall such a rainless year.

Jews, Moslems, and Christians alike became increasingly worried. The dread specter of famine now loomed in addition to the immediate water shortage problem. They gathered in their respective houses of prayer and prayed to the Al-mighty for mercy on the Holy City and its inhabitants. The rabbis of Jerusalem proclaimed days of fasting and special prayers. Hundreds of Jews made the excursion to the tomb of Rachel the Matriarch to light candles and pray for rain. Others went to the burial place of King David on nearby Mount Zion to beseech G-d's help there.

But, no rain. The cisterns had almost completely dried up, yet the heavenly sluices were still sealed shut. Not a cloud marred the perfectly blue sky. It was so close to springtime and the end of the rain season that many Jerusalemites were already girding themselves for a difficult, perhaps life threatening, period of famine and water shortage.

All the worries generated a stream of rumors, and the rumors in turn led to increased tension between the different ethnic groups in the holy city. The Arabs started to blame the Jews for the lack of rain. This obvious choice for scapegoat required no accompanying reason or explanation for its acceptance to quickly spread throughout the Muslim community, and quickly became an absolute certainty in all their minds.

The instigation against the Jews eventually reached the palace of the *pasha*, the governor, of the Jerusalem district of the Ottoman Empire. Indeed, certain Jew-haters made it a point to repeatedly bring this 'information' to his attention.

Soon thereafter, the *pasha* (Turkish governor) summoned the famed scholar and kabbalist, **Rabbi Moshe Galante**, who had moved from Tzefat to Jerusalem around 1655 C.E., and was now one of Jerusalem's leading rabbis, to appear before him. The rabbi entered with foreboding. Sure enough, his fears were realized when the pasha said, "I know that it is solely because of you Jews that G-d has not let it rain in Jerusalem. You people like to glorify yourselves that you are his chosen people; you call Him 'Father' and refer to yourselves as 'His children.' Therefore you are totally to blame.

"So I am warning you. You people had better pray seriously to your god. If it doesn't rain by the end of three days, it will be clear that it is all the fault of the Jews. I shall expel every single one of you from Jerusalem."

As soon as Rabbi Galante left the palace, he called an emergency meeting in the main synagogue, emphasizing that all the Jewish residents of Jerusalem should attend.

Everybody came. Their faces reflected their worry over the situation. The whole population knew that Rabbi Galante had been summoned to the governor. When he informed them what had transpired, they groaned under this new burden. Was the trial of thirst they had already started to undergo not enough? Now they also had to have the wrath of the pasha and the entire Arab population hovering over them?

Rabbi Galante declared a three-day fast, with the time to be spent in prayer and pleading before the Al-mighty, in the hope of abolishing the evil decree.

A spirit of gloom descended upon the Jews of Jerusalem as the possibility of expulsion from the Holy City loomed over them. With broken hearts and flowing tears, they crowded together in the shuls to recite Psalms and pray for mercy from Above. Many also went to stand before *the Western Wall* and exert themselves in further supplications. 'G-d, have pity on Your poor suffering people in Your Holy City.'

One day passed, and a second. On the third day the skies were as blue and cloudless as ever. Dread descended upon the hearts of all the Jews, men, women and children, and further stimulated their prayers. They were hungry and thirsty, and still fasting; surely their desperate cries pierced through all the heavens.

The sun marched inexorably across the sky, and now stood in the western sector of the sky. The final hours of the afternoon were slowly dwindling. Rabbi Galante announced that everyone should proceed together outside the city walls to the tomb of *Shimon HaTzadik*, the great sage and high priest from the early years of the Second Temple, and there to pray one last time for rain. He also made another demand that startled all that were present. Nobody could believe what they imagined they had heard.

What he said was that everyone should put on their galoshes or boots, wear raincoats, and have umbrellas in hand! Why? Lest they get drenched in the expected downpour!

Despite their shock and amazement, everyone complied faithfully. At the designated time, the Jews of Jerusalem left the city through Damascus Gate, dressed in their boots and raincoats, and carrying umbrellas. When the police officer in charge of the area saw this strange parade, he burst into laughter, but then, when he heard they were marching through the streets dressed in their raingear only because their rabbi had ordered them to do so and promised them a heavy rainstorm, he became furious. He caught up to the rabbi, slapped him severely in the face, and screamed, "The people of the city are suffering so much, and you dare to waste their time and strength in such foolishness!"

Rabbi Galante did not respond, and kept walking.

When they arrived at the gravesite, the rabbi prostrated himself on the tombstone and remained there, immersed in profound concentration. All the other people cried out in prayer from the depths of their hearts.

Suddenly, they realized that a breeze was blowing—a soft, gentle breeze, but still a breeze! Then, rather quickly, the breeze became a real wind, which began to blow furiously. A storm wind!

The sky turned grey and filled with dark clouds. A few raindrops were felt. Then it began to drizzle, and soon after that to pour. The Jews opened their umbrellas. In no time at all, they were in the midst of a torrential shower. They joyfully hurried to take shelter under trees and next to the nearby houses.

Peering through the deluge, they saw to their surprise a man running as fast as he could in the rain towards them. It was the police officer! By the time he reached them, he was so thoroughly soaked he seemed to be made more of water than of solid flesh. He made straight for Rabbi Galante and threw himself down in the mud before his feet. "Forgive me, please, for how I insulted you," he begged. "I didn't realize you were such a great, holy person."

In order to display his sincerity and make amends, he lifted the rabbi onto his shoulders, marched with him at the head of the Jewish procession back to town, and carried him all the way to the door of his house.

The rainstorm continued all the night. By dawn, all the cisterns were filled to overflowing. Later in the morning, the pasha himself came and apologized for threatening to expel the Jews. He proffered more words of appeasement and then stated emotionally, "Now I know that your L-rd is the true G-d, and that you Jews really are his treasured people."

Source: Translated-adapted by Yerachmiel Tilles from the Hebrew weekly *Sichat Hashavua*, #204. (First published on *AscentOf Safed com.*)

PART TWO

Chasidic Masters: First Three Generations

1734–1815 (C.E.)

Happy Birthday! 5

PART 2
5
18th Century (middle) Eastern Europe

Biographical notes for this story:

Rabbi **Yisrael ben Eliezer** [of blessed memory: 18 Elul 5458– 6 Sivan 5520 (August 1698– May 1760 C.E.)], the ***Baal Shem Tov*** ["master of the good Name" — often referred to as "the ***Besht***" for short], a unique and seminal figure in Jewish history, revealed his identity as an exceptionally holy person, on his 36th birthday, 18 Elul 5494 (1734 C.E.), and made the until-then underground chasidic movement public. He wrote no books, although many claim to contain his teachings. One available in English is the excellent annotated translation of *Tzava'at Harivash*, published by Kehos.

This story can be related to:

Weekly Readings: *Toldot* — Genesis 27:11–12, 15–16 ("She [Rebecca] placed young goat's skins on his [Jacob's] arms and on the hairless parts of his neck"; *Vayakhel* — Exodus 35:26 ("Highly skilled women spun the goats' wool" — on the live goats — *Rashi*)

The Jewish Holidays: *Shavuot*

Jewish Calendar Date: *Sivan* 6 (*Shavuot*) — *yahrzeit* of the *Besht*; *Elul* 18 (12 days before *Rosh Hashana*) — birthday of *Besht* (1698) and anniversary of his revealing the chasidic movement (1734).

Main Themes: Birthdays, Belief in rebbes

Other Topics: Wives, Debts, Non-Jews, Buying-selling, Marketplace, Anti-semitism

Happy Birthday!

A JEW WHO HAD LEASED the rights to a certain enterprise on the estates of *Graff* [Duke] Putatski found himself in deep trouble. Business had been very slow, and now he was two years in arrears on the lease-money to an impatient and cruel landlord. The duke threatened him that if he didn't pay the whole debt by the end of the month when the third year would begin, he would toss him and his wife and children into a dungeon and leave them there to rot. There wasn't a question in the poor Jew's mind that the duke was prepared to keep his word.

But where was he to get the money? Business was still terrible, and he didn't know anyone from whom he could borrow such a large sum. The days passed. He felt tormented, and his wife and children were terrified and in tears, but he couldn't come up with a workable idea. True, his wife had suggested going for advice and blessing to the so-called wonder-making rabbi who lived not far across the border, but that was patently ridiculous. Perhaps it was permitted for the naive and the uneducated to believe the stories told about the Baal Shem Tov, but **he** was a G-d-fearing Torah scholar. It was not proper for him to go near such a person.

As the final week drew near, he was no closer to a solution. His wife kept insisting he go to the Baal Shem Tov. Finally, in desperation, and to find some relief from her tearful entreaties, he agreed to make the journey. So what if he talked to the man. It didn't mean he had to follow his advice.

Upon being ushered into the Baal Shem Tov's room, he recounted his whole sad story. The Rebbe's response took him by surprise.

"Sunday morning, go to town, to the market area. When a gentile peasant approaches you and offers to sell you something he has, accept immediately. Pay no attention to what it is, how it looks, or whether it is worth the price he asks. Just buy it. Then come here again and I'll tell you what to do with it."

He returned home and reported to his wife what the Baal Shem Tov had said, and announced scornfully that he had no intention whatsoever of wasting his time and doing it. His wife, however, who believed in wonders and miracles, made sure that on that Sunday morning he set out for town.

Feeling ridiculous, he strolled around the deserted square. Suddenly, a farmer appeared and asked him if he would like to buy something nice, and showed him the sheepskin that he was holding. He asked how much it would cost him and was told, one gold coin. It was exactly what he had in his pocket, the last of his money! Astonished to his depths by the series of seeming coincidences that exactly matched what the Baal Shem Tov had told him, he handed over the gold piece to the farmer without thinking further about it and took possession of the wooly skin.

"Wait a minute!" he kicked himself. "What did I do? The last of my money for a sheepskin? Am I crazy? I can't believe I did this," and he ran quickly through the streets to find the gentile who had fleeced him, but he couldn't find him. The peasant had disappeared as eerily as he had come. He felt depressed and aggravated.

When he arrived home, he exploded at his wife, "It's all **your** fault. **You** made me do this. What good can this silly fleece possibly do? And now we have no money at all."

She remained calm. She simply commented that the entire episode constituted a confirmation that the wondrous rabbi knew exactly what he was talking about. Had not every word he said come true? "Stop being so stubborn," she told him. "You know that many important rabbis also go to consult the

Baal Shem Tov. Just go back to him and see what he said to do with the sheepskin."

What choice did he have? Once more he traveled to the Baal Shem Tov. He told him in a bitter tone what had happened that Sunday. The Rebbe gave him a wide smile. "You did very well, my friend," he said. "Now listen to what you should do next.

The birthday of your Graff will occur in a few days. He'll throw a huge party for all his aristocratic friends. Each of them will of course bring him a birthday gift appropriate to their stature. You too should show up that day and bring him a present, the sheepskin!"

The man could not believe his ears. Was the Baal Shem Tov teasing him, making fun of his situation? He hurried home and shouted at his wife that her precious rabbi had advised him to commit suicide.

"Don't be ridiculous," she responded.

"It's true," he retorted. After quoting to her the Baal Shem Tov's words, he added morosely, "Picture what would happen if I were to follow his absurd plan. The lords of the land will come, bringing with them the most precious items available in honor of the duke: fine wines, rare fruits, valuable jewels. You name it. Then I stroll in and offer him a ragged sheepskin. Is there any doubt that he will promptly have me executed for the insult? Of course he will. Not only that, we have to be afraid about repercussions of his wrath on the rest of the Jewish community too."

His wife dismissed his fears. "Don't try to understand what is not possible to fathom. All you have to do is carry out the rabbi's instructions exactly. Be courageous, and strengthen your faith in G-d Al-mighty and His righteous ones."

The day came. It was the duke's birthday, and only a few days until his final deadline. He woke with a sinking feeling in his stomach. Sure enough, that afternoon his wife insisted that he go to the duke and present him the sheepskin. Unable to think of any alternative, either good or bad, he realized he would have to go. He set out, walking slowly, his heart beating wildly.

As he approached the property, his apprehension grew even more. By the time he was in sight of the manor, he was terrified. Beads of sweat dotted his forehead. He had to force himself to take each succeeding step. As he came closer, he could see numerous fancy carriages of the guest nobility.

He stood at the door, but could not bring himself to knock. "Should I really do it?" he debated with himself, "Or should I just go home?" He finally decided that only evil could befall him there, and turned to start home.

At that moment the door swung upon, and one of the duke's guards emerged. Spotting the tenant, he shouted, "Jew! What do you want here?"

He couldn't respond. He opened his mouth, but just couldn't force himself to say the words that he had brought a present for the duke. Nevertheless, somehow the man guessed his intention, and said, "Perhaps you brought a present for the master. What's that in your hand?"

Still speechless, he extended his arm so that the guard could see the sheepskin. The latter whooped in derision. He took the fleece in one hand and grabbed the Jew's arm with the other, and marched him into the oversized dining hall where the duke was entertaining his noble guests. "Your Highness, look how your wretched Jew insults you. This is his disgusting "gift" for you on your special day."

Taking in the sheepskin in a quick glance, the duke's first reaction was shock, which quickly gave way to fury. "Take him off to the dungeon until I have time to deal with this," he commanded his servants. "Why should I let him ruin a good party."

He went to rejoin his guests in their drinking and carousing, but somehow it wasn't the same. He couldn't get the incident of the sheepskin out of his mind. "Sure, Jews are greedy and sly and disloyal," he mused to himself; "everybody knows that. But stupid? No. Not at all. So why did the Jew endanger his life with that worthless piece of fleece? There must be more to this than is apparent."

He decided to take a few minutes to think the matter over in private. Excusing himself to his guests, he retired to his den, hauling the strange gift with him. Maybe there was something special about it and he hadn't looked closely enough. Indeed, he now noticed that a bit of the wool on one side was curled in the shape of a letter. And next to it was another letter. And another, and another! It was unbelievable! The fleece lay in such a way that it spelled his name, his father's name, his family name, and the year, month, and date of his birth!

Duke Putatsky stared and stared at the wonder in his hand. He couldn't get over it. Could some craftsman actually have done this? Could it possibly be natural?

Snapping out of his joyous reverie, he ran back to the main room and went from table to table, excitedly showing his prize to his guests, and asking them what they thought. They too were thoroughly amazed by the phenomenon. His question, however, presented no difficulty. There could not possibly exist in the world a craftsman who could accomplish such a wonder; it must be unnatural, a miracle from heaven. "But perhaps we are being hasty," a few of them remarked. "Why don't you ask your Jew where he acquired it?"

"Of course," exclaimed the duke, clapping his hands. "That's what I should have done right off." He quickly sent someone to fetch his tenant from the dungeon.

"Where did you get this skin?" the duke demanded.

The poor man was convinced his end had come. He threw himself on the floor at the feet of the duke and begged for mercy. "It's not my fault," he cried. "A weird rabbi told me to do it. My wife made me do it." Sobbing uncontrollably, he told them the whole story.

"Relax, my good fellow," said the duke kindly. "Don't be afraid. Your rabbi is indeed a holy man. It is a blessing for me and you that he sent you here. What seemed to be a worthless skin is to me now the most precious, valuable item in the world."

The Jew couldn't believe his ears. The duke showed him the extraordinary wonder of the names and dates embedded in the fleece. "I'm so pleased with you," he said to his astonished tenant, "that I relinquish all of your debt, and in return for your unique present to me, I have several nice gifts for you."

Smiling, the duke handed the Jew some extremely expensive objects of gold and silver. Many of the wealthy guests also bestowed upon him money and valuable presents. He left there no longer a poor man, and from that day on all his business efforts prospered, and he became quite wealthy.

Only one question remained. What should be done with the miraculous sheepskin? The nobles discussed it for a while, and decided that the duke should make a wool hat out of it, and every year on his birthday he should wear it and display it. Together with that, he should also be sure to give a suitably expensive gift to the Jew, in gratitude for his having given him the best birthday present ever, beyond anyone's imagining.

Source: Translated and freely adapted by Yerachmiel Tilles from *Sipurei Chasidim-Torah* (#216) by Rabbi S. Y. Zevin. (First published on *AscentOf Safed.com*.)

6 Beyond Space

Biographical notes for this story:

Rabbi **Dov Ber** [of blessed memory: c.5460– 19 Kislev 5533 (c.1700–Dec. 1772 C.E.)], the son of Avraham and Chava, known as the ***Maggid of Mezritch***, succeeded his master, the *Baal Shem Tov*, as the head of the chasidic movement. Most of the leading chasidic dynasties stem from his disciples and his descendents. The classic anthologies of his teachings are *Likutei Amarim* and *Torah Ohr* (combined by Kehas Publishing as *Maggid Devorav l'Yaakov*), and *Ohr HaEmmes*.

6

18th Century (2nd half) Eastern Europe

This story can be related to:

Weekly Readings: *Trumah* — the Table, the Menorah and the Ark in the *Mishkan* — Sanctuary: Exodus 25:10–40; *Vayakhel* — Exodus 37:1–24 (these two readings usually occur in the weeks before and after Purim respectively).

The Jewish Holidays: *Yud-Tes Kislev* (A chasidic celebration — especially Chabad)

Jewish Calendar Date: Kislev 19 (week before Chanukah) — *yahrzeit* of the Maggid of Mezritch

Main Themes: Opposition to chasidism, Wealth and poverty, Holy Temple;

Other Topics: Chasid-Rebbe, Buying-selling, Humility

Beyond Space

In the time of the great Maggid, there lived in Mezritch a Jewish householder who was both wealthy and an accomplished Torah scholar. He was able to devote most of his time to Torah study and prayer. His wife ran the store that belonged to them, and he had to be there only two hours a day. The rest of his time was spent in the *Beit Midrash* (house of study) learning Torah.

This man was opposed to the chasidic movement and, as a result, had never gone to visit the Maggid. One Friday morning, he came very early to the Beit Midrash and saw several young men sitting there studying. It seemed they had been there most of the night. He didn't recognize any of them and realized that they had to be from out of town.

He went over to greet them with the traditional *Shalom Aleichem*, and conversed with them a bit, asking them where they were from and why they had come. They told him they had journeyed from afar to see the 'Rebbe'.

Their reply made him think. "People travel here from great distances to see the Maggid, while I, who live here in Mezritch, have never gone to see him even once. I really should do so, at least one time."

He thought some more. "Of course, I cannot justify interrupting my Torah studies for such a thing, but I suppose I can skip going to the shop for one day." And that is what he did.

When he entered the Maggid's room, he was immediately struck by the Maggid's holy appearance and the divine illumination that seemed to radiate from him.

After that first encounter, he began to visit the Maggid

more and more, even relinquishing some of his study sessions in order to do so. He eventually became totally attached to the Maggid as his Rebbe, heart and soul, just like the other devoted chasidim.

Then, after a while, his business took a downward turn. As time went by, the decline became even more serious. His affairs continued to deteriorate until he was nearly impoverished.

He couldn't understand why this should have happened to him. Hadn't he increased his merit in the eyes of heaven by becoming a follower of the great Maggid? But wait! It seemed that the beginning of his economic downfall could be traced to when he became a chasid!

He decided to present this burning question to his holy teacher. The Maggid answered him, "As a scholar you must know what it says in the Talmud [*Berachot*]. 'Whoever wishes to be wise should face south [in prayer]. Whoever wishes to be wealthy should face north.* For the Menorah was positioned in the south and the Showbread Table stood in the north.'

"So let me ask you. What if someone wishes to be both wise and wealthy? There is a vast distance between north and south!"**

The man didn't know what to answer. He waited silently.

The Maggid continued. "If a person makes himself as if he is nothing, then he becomes a spiritual entity. As that which is spiritual takes no space and is not restricted by space, he can then be both here and there."***

These words penetrated the new chasid's heart. He worked on himself to become much more humble, shedding his scholar's haughtiness. As he did so, he found that his business took an upward turn, and it was not long until he was wealthy once again, as he had been initially.

Source: Translated and freely adapted by Yerachmiel Tilles from *Sipurei Chasidim-Torah* (#216) by Rabbi S. Y. Zevin. (First published on *AscentOf Safed.com.*)

Translator's notes:

—

* Can also be translated as "go south ... go north." Actually, the quote uses both 'north' and 'south' as verbs; both the 'pray' or the 'go' are not literally there.

** Also, we face Jerusalem when we pray, we do not have a choice of directions.

*** The Torah reading of Trumah discusses not only the Menorah and the Showbread Table, but also the Ark of the Law. If we examine its measurements against those of the opening to the "Holy of Holies" inner sanctuary carefully, we find that it could not logically fit!

Biographical note for this story:

Rabbi **Yisrael ben Eliezer** [of blessed memory: 18 Elul 5458– 6 Sivan 5520 (Aug. 1698– May 1760 C.E.)], the ***Baal Shem Tov*** ["master of the good Name" — often referred to as "the *Besht*" for short], a unique and seminal figure in Jewish history, revealed his identity as an exceptionally holy person, on his 36th birthday, 18 Elul 5494 (1734 C.E.), and made the until-then underground chasidic movement public. He wrote no books, although many claim to contain his teachings. One available in English is the excellent annotated translation of *Tzava'at Harivash*, published by Kehos.

7
18th Century (middle) Eastern Europe

This story can be related to:

Weekly Readings: *Shmot* — Exodus 1:1 ("And these are the names of the children of Israel..." although the name of the parsha and the entire book for that matter means "Names"); *Vayetzei* — Genesis 29:32–35, 30:5–13, 17–24 (naming of 11 sons and 1 daughter).

The Jewish Holidays: Shavuot

Jewish Calendar Date: Sivan 6 (*Shavuot*) — *yahrzeit* of the *Besht*; Elul 18 (12 days before *Rosh Hashana*) — his birth-date (1698) and anniversary of his revealing the chasidic movement (1734)

Main Themes: Naming, Birthing, Education

Other Topics: Children

Popular Names

MOSHE SHLOMO, a village merchant, was a simple, good-hearted person, as was his wife Rivka. They always gave generously to worthy charitable causes, including to the Baal Shem Tov for the support of the hidden tzadikim. Only one thing distressed them. Although they had been married for fifteen years they didn't have any children.

Many times during that decade and a half, Moshe Shlomo had gone to the Baal Shem Tov and entreated him to pray for them to have children. The Baal Shem Tov always showered him with blessings, for wealth, long life, health, and happiness, but never for what he so dearly hoped to hear.

The Baal Shem Tov's close disciples also asked their master for this blessing for the beloved Moshe Shlomo, but he never responded to them.

Ten more years went by. The Baal Shem Tov's blessings all came to fruition. Moshe Shlomo's business affairs prospered and expanded. The couple, however, grew even more unhappy. They still had no children, and no encouragement from the Rebbe, The Baal ShemTov.

One day, in the beginning of the week, they both went to see him. "Why do you two look so sad?" asked the Baal Shem Tov. Hasn't G-d blessed you with great prosperity, and good health? And you have made the most of these blessings to do many *mitzvos* and good deeds."

"All that you say may be true," they both answered, "but still, we have no children. What do we need all of this wealth for?" They burst into tears. "After 120, there will be no inheritor, no one to name chidren after us, and no one to remember us."

The Baal Shem Tov did not respond directly. He simply said, "Tomorrow I'm leaving on a little journey with a few of my students. Why don't you two come along also?"

They were surprised by the invitation, but they quickly agreed.

The travelers set out the next morning, in a line of carriages. For three days they were on the road, until finally they arrived at a little town. After a short rest, the Baal Shem Tov suggested that they all go out and have a look around.

As they walked, they came across a group of children playing in the sand. The Baal Shem Tov went over to them and said to the nearest one, "What's your name?"

"Boruch Moshe," the lad answered.

The Baal Shem Tov then asked another boy, and his name was also Boruch Moshe. The third one was Moshe Avraham, the fourth, Boruch Mordechai, and the fifth Boruch Moshe again. A little girl piped up, "And my name is Brocha Leah."

As they walked on, they came across a group of little girls. The Shem Tov asked them their names, and most of them turned out to be Brocha Leah too.

Next they entered a *cheder* [school for pre-bar mitzvah boys]. Six of the little boys were named Boruch Moshe, while most of the rest were Boruch or Moshe or one of those two names in combination with another. They went into a few more schools, and also a yeshiva that had students from all the surrounding villages, and found the same pattern of names. Not only that, the girls they encountered along the way were mostly named Brocha Leah, or one of those names singly or in combination with another.

Moshe Shlomo and Rivka were astonished, as were all the other disciples. How could it be that all these children had the same names? The Rebbe, however, seemed to be smiling in satisfaction, but none dared ask him for an explanation.

By now it was time for the afternoon *Mincha* prayer. The men went into a shul. As soon as the *minyan* [prayer quorem of 10 men] ended, the Baal Shem Tov asked one of the local men why all the children of the town had the same names. The man answered obligingly that he would be happy to tell them the whole story. The disciples craned their necks in eager anticipation, expecting to hear about a great tzadik or outstanding scholar who had lived in these parts.

"Boruch Moshe was born in this town nearly one hundred years ago," the man began. "His father, Isaac-Shalom, was an accomplished Torah scholar who made a good living as a butcher. He was known for his generosity.

"His one frustration was that his son, Boruch Moshe, seemed to have no flair for learning Torah whatsoever. In consequence, he left yeshiva at age fifteen and began to help his father in his butcher shop. He picked up this work quickly and easily. As he grew older, his father turned over more and more of the business to him, and after seeing his son succeed, retired to devote most of his time to Torah study.

"When the time came, Boruch Moshe married Brocha Leah, whose good nature and kindheartedness were similar to his. Years went by. The couple was not blessed with offspring. When Boruch Moshe's parents passed away, he wanted to learn Mishna for the benefit of their souls, but he didn't know how. He hired a teacher, a known scholar named Shlomo-Yitzchak, but it didn't help. He just couldn't seem to assimilate the minimal necessary skills.

"He felt terrible. He wasn't able to learn Torah for his dear departed parents, and he didn't have any children that would be able to do so for him and his wife after 120 either.

"Once, when he was sitting in shul, he overheard something from the daily Talmud class. The Rabbi read aloud, 'If someone teaches his friend's son Torah, it is as if he gave birth to him.'

"That made him feel even worse. Not only did he not have children of his own, but he didn't have the ability to 'acquire' others by teaching them Torah either. When the study session ended, Boruch Moshe asked the Rabbi if he could speak with him privately, and poured out his heart to him.

"'No, no, my friend,' the Rabbi said gently, 'you didn't understand completely. One doesn't have to teach the children directly in order to merit being considered their parent. It is enough to arrange and provide for their education.'

"As the explanation sank in, the darkness in Boruch Moshe's heart dissipated, replaced by a bright burning light. When he told Brocha Leah, she was also ecstatic. They went out and hired thirty tutors, for all the children in the town and surrounding villages who didn't yet have one.

"Boruch Moshe's meat business prospered and he actually became quite wealthy, but he and his wife continued in their same modest lifestyle; all their money was dedicated to Torah education.

"I, my brothers, and all our friends attended the cheder of Boruch Moshe," the smiling man concluded his story, "and so did the Rabbi of the town. Boruch Moshe and Brocha Leah both passed away fifteen years ago. Out of deep feelings of gratitude and a desire to memorialize them, we all named our sons and daughters after this extraordinary couple. On their yahrzeits, the Rabbi says the *Kaddish* prayer for their souls, and a large crowd of former students whom they supported visit their graves, just as children do for their parents."

The Baal Shem Tov, his followers, and the couple thanked the man and prepared themselves for the return trip. Everyone understood quite clearly the lesson of their journey, especially Moshe Shlomo and Rivka. Now they knew how to preserve their names in a most desirable and meritorious manner. The same day they arrived home, they hired some teachers for the poor children of their town. Dozens of children were now able to learn Torah as a result of their generosity and dedication.

In the next generation, if you were to have visited that town and encountered large numbers of children named Moshe Shlomo and Rivka, surely you would not be surprised.

Source: Translated-adapted by Yerachmiel Tilles from the Hebrew weekly *Sichat HaShavua*, #130. (First published in *Ascent Quarterly* #19 — also printed in *Kfar Chabad* #819.) Recently supplemented with some factual details printed in "*The Great Mission*" (Kehot).

8 The Forest and the Rose

8

18th Century (2nd half) Eastern Europe

Biographical notes for this story:

Rabbi **Leib Sarah's** [of blessed memory: 5490– 4 Adar-a 5556 (1730–Feb. 1796 C.E.)] was held in high esteem by the Baal Shem Tov. One of the society of hidden "tzadikim" (purely righteous), he spent his life wandering from place to place to raise money for the ransoming of imprisoned Jews and the support of other hidden tzadikim.

Rabbi **Yitzchak-Isaac Taub** of Kaliv [of blessed memory: 5504– 7 Adar-b 5581 (1744– March 1821 C.E.)] was an orphan goat-herder in his youth until he was "discovered" by Reb Leib Sarah's and brought to study under Rabbi Shmuel-Shmelke in Nicholsburg, an important follower of the Maggid of Mezritch. Subsequently he also studied under another major follower of the Maggid, Rebbi Elimelech of Lizhinsk (see the bio note story #11). He was a seminal figure in the spreading of chasidism in Hungary, and was known for the beautiful lyrics he composed in Hungarian for ancient tunes.

This story can be related to:

Weekly Readings: *Vayigash* — Genesis 47:14 ("Yosef gathered in all the silver that was found in the Land of Egypt." Kabbalah interpretation: Yosef sought out and purified all the sparks of sanctity which were scattered throughout Egypt, separated them from their worldly husks, and elevated them.)

Jewish Calendar Date: *Adar-a*, 4 — yahrzeit of Rabbi Leib Sarah's (two weeks after Tu b'Shvat); *Adar-b*, 7 (one week before Purim) — yahrzeit of the first Kaliver Rebbe.

Main Themes: Song, Hidden tzadikim

Other Topics: Music, Divine sparks, Becoming a chasid, Education

The Forest and the Rose

SHABBAT HAD ENDED. Silver stars twinkled in the black sky. The chasidim had all returned to their homes, and their Rebbe, **Leib Sarah's** (called so because of the extraordinary deeds of his mother Sarah and the exceptional circumstances surrounding his birth, but that's a story for another time) left his shul for home to conduct *havdalah* [ceremony marking the end of Shabbat] for his family.

Shortly after, he returned to the shul. Agitated, he paced back and forth, muttering "Oy, Oy" over and over again. Suddenly he stood still, and a tremor shuddered through his body. "Whatever happens," he stated with finality, "I must do something."

Stepping outside, he summoned his driver. In a short time they were off. The tzadik whispered something in the driver's ear, and then switched places with him, taking over the reins while the driver went to sleep inside the carriage. When the coachman woke, the sun had already risen on Sunday morning, and he was amazed to discover how far they had come. Being the regular driver for the *tzadik*, he had experience in these miraculous-seeming journeys, but this time he could barely believe the evidence of his eyes. They had actually crossed the border and were deep into Hungary!

Little Isaac was only ten years old, but was already the man of the house. His father, Yusseleh, had recently passed away, and his mother Reizel desperately needed him to help support the family. She took whatever meager work was available to her, while little Isaac took care of their tiny flock of goats.

Actually, Isaac liked his job. Every morning he rose early to pray with the *minyan* in shul and say *Kaddish* for his father. He would then lead the goats to one of the fields outside of town. He loved the quiet and peace there. After carefully counting his meager charges, he would sit against the trunk of a tree and enjoy the cool shade under its big, leafy branches.

Many thoughts would race through his little head, some joyous, some sad. In those moments when his young soul was bursting with a variety of different feelings, he would open his knapsack and seek the soothing comfort provided by his beloved flute. Quickly he would extract from it a medley of folk tunes, passed down from generation to generation in the Hungarian countryside, all learned from the other herdsmen that he encountered. Of his whole repertoire, his favorite song's words went:

Forest, forest, how vast you are.
Rose, oh rose, how far you are.
If the forest were but smaller,
Then the rose would be closer.
If you would take me from this forest,
Then we could be, the two of us, together.

Whenever he played the notes of this tune, he would close his eyes and allow the lyrics and the music to carry him off to a world of distant pleasant visions.

Isaac was startled in the midst of his song, by the regal appearance of the bearded Jew who appeared suddenly from behind him. "What are you doing here, little boy?" the man asked gently. "Helping my mother by tending our goats," Isaac answered. “But what about learning Torah in school like the other boys?” the man continued.

Isaac looked away. “Not so long ago, I was still a student, and I was doing pretty well too, but ever since my father died, I’ve had to help my poor mother support our family.”

The Tzadik Leib Sarah’s immediately went to visit the poor widow, Reizel. After introducing himself, he asked her for permission to take her Isaac away with him. “Know that your son has a very lofty soul,” he explained, “and he can become very great, but for that he must be brought up in the right way, and that means he has to study Torah intensively.” He promised her a monthly stipend to more than make up for any loss of income that the boy’s departure would entail.

It took a lot of entreating, but finally his mother agreed. Leib Sarah’s took little Isaac to Nicholsberg, to the Yeshiva of the great rabbinical authority and Chasidic Rebbe, Reb Shmelke, a friend of Leib Sarah’s and one of the inner circle of disciples of the Magid of Mezritch. He said to him, “I have brought you a special soul from the Chamber of Melody. I hope you will help it to realize its full potential in this world.”

Isaac remained in the Nicholsberg Yeshiva for many years, and thrived and grew great in Torah and Chasidut.

Years later, when throngs of chasidim would crowd into the shul of their holy rebbe, Rabbi **Yitzchak Isaac of Kaliv**, he would sometimes relate to them the long path of his development from a goat-herding childhood to the present. On these occasions, he always mentioned his great debt to the Tzadik Leib Sarah’s, who went to such trouble to discover him and help him.

He also liked to tell them about his favorite tune that he played regularly on his shepherd’s flute, “The Ballad of the Forest and the Rose”, which turned out to be a holy melody that had been languishing in captivity for centuries.

"Now, however," he would always conclude, "the tune is redeemed and the words are different." The chasidim would listen intently, for the Rebbe's musical talents were well-known.

Exile, exile, how long you are.
*Shechinah, *Shechinah, how far you are.*
If only the exile were shorter,
Then Your Presence could be closer.
If You would take us out of exile,
Then we could be, the two of us, together.

This song is still sung by Kaliver chasidim, in Hungarian, till this very day. Indeed, here is a link to it and a related song being sung by the current Kaliver Rebbe!: ** www.youtube.com/watch?v=DuTuKufvgO4

Source: Translated and freely adapted by Yerachmiel Tilles from the Hebrew weekly *Sichat HaShavua*, #528. (First published in *Kfar Chabad Magazine* #762 — the inaugural edition containing an English supplement in 5757/1997!)***

Translator's notes:

—

* Divine Presence

** The video link was first sent to me by my dear friend Yosef Ben Shlomo HaKohen (nee Jeff Obler), May he rest in peace.

*** This story is the first one I ever published professionally!

To See the Rebbe's Face

Biographical notes for this story:

Rabbi **Menachem Mendel of Vitebsk/Horodok** [1730– 1 Iyar 1788 C.E.] was an elder disciple of the *Maggid of Mizritch* successor to the *Baal Shem Tov,* and one of the earliest chasidic rebbes. He led the first modern aliyah to Israel, in 1777 C.E., where he and three hundred chasidim and others settled in Tzefat (Safed). After a few years they moved to Tiberias. He is buried there in the Students of the Baal Shem Tov section of the Old Cemetery. His works include *Pri HaAretz* and *Likutei Amarim.*

Rabbi **Menachem Mendel Schneersohn** [29 Elul 1789– 13 Nissan 1866 C.E.], the third Rebbe of Chabad, was known as the ***Tzemach Tzedek***, after his books of Halachic responsa and Talmudic commentary (called by that name). He was renowned not only as a Rebbe, but also as a leading scholar in his generation in both the revealed and hidden aspects of Torah.

This story can be related to:

Weekly Readings: *Tazria* — Leviticus 12:3 ("On the eighth day, his foreskin shall be circumcised"); *Yitro* — Exodus 20:8 ("Remember the Shabbat [in order] to sanctify it"); *Lech Lecha* Genesis 17:10–12 (covenant of circumcision).

Jewish Calendar Date: *Iyar* 1 (1 week after the end of Pesach) — *yahrzeit* of R. Menachem-Mendel of Vitebsk / Horodok

Main Themes: Shabbat, Purity of Torah study

Other Topics: Circumcision, Chasid-Rebbe, Spirit of impurity

To See the Rebbe's Face

—

ONCE, the *Tsemach Tsedek* (the third *Chabad* Rebbe) emerged from his room and entering the Study Hall, found one of the young men looking at a small book in his lap instead of the large tome of Talmud on his desk.

"What is this book?" the Rebbe asked gently.

"*Pri HaAretz*, from the Vitebsker," was the answer.

"Rabbi **Menachem Mendel of Horodok**!"* the Rebbe shouted. "Quick! Light more candles. Light! More light!"

When someone finally worked up the nerve to ask the Rebbe for an explanation for his seemingly bizarre behavior, he offered to tell them a story, much to the delight of the young men and everyone else there.

In Horodok lived a *shochet* (kosher slaughterer) and expert *mohel* (one who performs circumcision) who was a close follower of Rabbi Menachem Mendel. Once he was invited to be the mohel at a *brit milah* (circumcision ceremony) in a nearby village. Since the brit was scheduled to take place early on Friday morning, he would be able to return in plenty of time for Shabbat. On the way back, however, he got lost when somehow he strayed from the path that went through the thick forest.

After a long time of wandering about, he realized sadly that he wouldn't be able to make it home before Shabbat. Soon after, he saw in the distance a shining light. Immediately he set out in that direction, and as he got closer, he saw a house. He went in, and to his surprise found a large minyan of majestically attired men about to begin the Shabbat evening prayers. He joined in and enjoyed their prayer service very much.

Afterwards he followed them into the next room, and soon

there was a crowd of men sitting around a long table beautifully set for Shabbat, and a distinguished-looking old man with a long white beard was at its head. For the duration of the meal, the elder expounded Torah, and when he did everyone listened intently.

The chasid listened too, and was quite impressed by the brilliant insights. From time to time, one of the listeners seated near him would whisper, "*Nu*? How do you like our Rabbi's words of Torah? Do you approve?"

"Yes!" The chasid answered each one enthusiastically.

The same scene repeated itself at the two Shabbat day mealswhenever new Torah insights were said, and he found the daytime Torah lessons even more intriguing than the ones from the night.

On Saturday night, after *Havdalah* (the ceremony marking the end of Shabbat), he found himself alone, so he left and made his way home, arriving quite late at night.

The mohel's custom was to go to his Rebbe's house every day, in order to pray in his minyan and to gaze upon his face. The Rebbe, for his part, was always pleased to see him.

That Sunday morning he went as early as he could. This time, however, the Rebbe's attendant did not allow him to enter. He was shocked, but not discouraged. Then again, at the time of the evening prayer, and on Monday and Tuesday too, he was refused entrance.

Three full days meant he could no longer dismiss the situation as temporary. He demanded from the attendant, "What is going on? Why won't you allow me to see the Rebbe?"

"Because the Rebbe told me not to."

"Oh, no!" exclaimed the chasid in dismay. "Why not? What could possibly be the reason?"

The attendant continued to insist that he didn't know why. The chasid cried and fasted and berated himself for much of the rest of the week. On Friday he returned to the door of the Rebbe's house and knocked and knocked until finally the attendant opened it a crack. "What are you doing here?" he asked brusquely. "How many times do I have to tell you that you are not allowed in?"

The chasid begged him with tears in his eyes. "Please, have mercy on me! Ask the Rebbe what I did to offend him so. What is my sin to deserve such a terrible punishment, to be denied access to the Rebbe?"

The attendant went in, and soon returned with a reply. "The Rebbe said to tell you that house in the forest belongs to the Evil Forces. Since you approved and accepted their words, you became connected to them and contaminated by them. Therefore, he cannot admit you in his presence."

The chasid was crushed. "But how can I live without seeing the Rebbe's holy face? Surely the Rebbe must know how I can rectify this. Please, please go to his room and ask him what I must do."

Back came the answer, "You have to go again before Shabbat to that forest and find that house. Then, each time they expound Torah and ask your opinion, you should express strong disapproval and spit. That is the only way you can escape their clutches. Be aware that it will be very difficult."

The mohel spent another week in self-examination and self-improvement, and on Friday afternoon set out with determination. He found the house in the forest, and the same people were sitting around the same table with the same elder again saying amazing words of Torah.

Again, some of the crowd approached him to ask what he thought. He hesitated momentarily, for the depth and creativity of the Torah was overwhelming, but then he thought of his beloved Rebbe and his wretched exile from him and regained control of himself. "*Feh, feh, feh*! Impure, impure, impure!" he screamed and spat emphatically.

Everyone froze. There was absolute silence. All heads turned towards him, and a few approached him menacingly.

"Wait," their leader said to them. He addressed the chasid,

"Who are you to dare to speak thus?"

"I am an insignificant nobody, but I am a follower of the holy Rebbe, Rabbi Menachem Mendel of Vitebsk and Horodok."

The old man turned again to his ranks. "Bring the record books," he exclaimed.

Then, addressing the chasid, he explained. "All the Torah expanations that were spoken and written with improper, self-serving intentions are contained there. If your Rebbe's name appears in our books, you are ours to do with as we wish. If not, we will be obligated to let you go."

A large number of identically bound thick volumes were brought out. Every page was turned and examined. Nowhere appeared the name of Rabbi Menachem Mendel of Horodok. Incredibly, he had never once wavered from learning Torah purely for the sake of G-d and His commandments.

The mohel left the house in the forest in peace, trembling in excited anticipation of his return to Horodok, and to once again be privileged to be with his Rebbe and to see his holy face.

"Now," concluded the Tsemek Tsedek with a smile, "you can understand that when the name of Rabbi Menachem Mendel of Horodok is mentioned, it is synonymous with great light."

Source: Translated by Yerachmiel Tilles from *Rishimat Devorim I* by Rabbi Yehuda Chitrik. But there the rebbe is Rabbi Ze'ev Wolf of Zhitomir, a different disciple of the Magid. However, I first heard this story from my first main Torah teacher and chasidic story master, Rabbi Akiva Greenberg of blessed memory, who said he heard it from the *Imrei Chaim* of Vizhnitz about Menachem Mendel of

Vitebsk, and I subsequently changed it accordingly and for this book added many details.**

Translator's notes:

—

* He was originally from Minsk, but after he became a disciple of the Maggid of Mezritch, he moved to Vitebsk. However, after less than a year there, the Maggid instructed him to move to Horodok, where he lived for over ten years until he led the chasidic *aliyah* to Israel. — Y.T.

** The shorter revised version was first published in *Under the Full Moon — Vol. 2, Winter* in 5770/ 2009, the 64 page booklet of 14 stories I produced for my younger son's wedding, which included earlier versions of 3 of the stories in this book. (Vol. 1 of *Under the Full Moon* came out in 5766/2006, in honor of my older son's wedding, in which only one of the twelve stories also appear here. Both volumes are available for purchase at //KabbalaOnline-shop.com.) The Zhitomir version was first published in *Kfar Chabad Magazine* #778 in 5758/1998.

10 "Enough Already!"

Biographical notes:

Rabbi **Menachem Nachum of Chernobyl** [of blessed memory: 5490–11 Cheshvan 5548 (1730–1787 C.E.)], was a disciple of the Baal Shem Tov and senior disciple of the Maggid of Mezritch. He is the author of *Meor Enayim.*

Rabbi **Mordechai ("Mottel") of Chernobyl** [of blessed memory: 5530– 20 Iyar 5697 (1770– May 1837 C.E.)], successor to his father, Rabbi Nachum, was the son-in-law of Rabbi Aharon the Great of Karlin, perhaps the most well-known follower of the Maggid in that generation, and subsequently of Rabbi **David Seirkes**, an important disciple of the Baal Shem Tov. His eight sons all became major chasidic leaders. One of them, Yaakov Yisrael Twerski of Cherkassy, the first Hornsteipel Rebbe, married Devora Leah, one of the six daughters of Rabbi DovBer of Lubavitch, son of Rabbi Shneur Zalman of Liadi (the match was arranged by the two grandfather-Rebbes), in order to maximize the possibilities for fulfillment of the prediction, "the *Moshiach* (Messiah) will be born of the elder disciple of the Maggid of Mezritch or the youngest."

10
18th Century
(2nd half)
Eastern Europe

This story can be related to:

Weekly Readings: *Tazria* — Leviticus 13 (all); *Mishpatim* — Exodus 21:1 ("These are the judgments..." — *Zohar*: "These are the reincarnations.")

Jewish Calendar Dates: *Cheshvan* 11 (a few weeks after *Simchat Torah*) — *yahrzeit* of Rebbe Nachum of Chernobyl; *Iyar* 20 (two days after *Lag b'Omer*) — *yahrzeit* of Rebbe Mottel of Chernobyl.

Main Themes: Suffering, Reincarnation

Other Topics: Skin disease, Mikveh, Wives

"Enough Already!"

THERE WAS A SERVANT in the house of the Tzadik, Rabbi **Mordechai ("Mottel'eh") of Chernobyl**, who used to stoke the fire in the winter stove. He was afflicted with severe psoriasis, and was covered from head to toe with painful boils and other skin eruptions. It seemed like he was always bleeding, either from the disease itself or from being unable to refrain from scratching at the relentless itching.

Whenever the Rebbe saw this servant, he never said a word about it to him, even though he undoubtedly noticed the young man's terrible suffering. His household and his chasidim were astonished, for the Rebbe's tremendous empathy for Jews in pain of any form was well-known to them.

One day, upon rising early in the morning, the Chernobyler came upon the servant crying and groaning in pain, furiously scratching at his head and other parts of his body, with blood oozing down from all over. The tzadik lifted his eyes and said, "Master of the Universe, let it be enough already!"

That same day, the servant suddenly died.

Now the Rebbe's household and the chasidim were even more amazed. Realizing that the turn of events was certainly out of the ordinary, they pleaded with the Rebbe for an explanation. Finally, he told them the following story.

Rabbi Motteleh's father, the famous Tzadik Rabbi Menachem Nachum of Chernobyl, was desperately poor. The family was always teetering on the brink of starvation. There was, however, a certain rich person in the town who loved the tzadik very much, and he used to provide the Rebbe with nearly all his household needs.

It came to pass that when this rich man realized how dear

he was to the Rebbe, it went to his head and he proposed to R. Nachum that the Tzadik's son marry his daughter. Of course, he would pay all the expenses of both sides as well as provide a handsome dowry, he confidently told the Chernobyler.

The Rebbe turned down his proposal.

The man continued to argue and plead his case, but the Rebbe was steadfast in his refusal. As a result, the man changed from the Tzadik's biggest supporter to his fiercest enemy. Not only did he cut off his financial aid, he actively sought to aggravate him, and was constantly inventing new plots to make the Chernobyler's life more difficult.

One time, he somehow found out that Rabbi Nachum's married daughter was due to go to the *mikveh* (ritual immersion pool) that night. His antagonism had so festered in him that he actually decided to hire some ruffians to pursue her through the streets on her way home afterwards. They did so in a brutish obnoxious way, and she was forced to flee with all her might through narrow side streets and filthy back alleys. Finally she reached the haven of her home, exhausted and upset. She crossed the threshold, collapsed on the floor, and fainted.

A great commotion arose in the Rebbe's home. Only after immense effort was the household able to bring her back to herself. When Rabbi Nachum found out that his daughter's suffering was a result of the rich man's evil plan, he was furious.

Shortly thereafter, the rich man died.

When the wealthy man's case came before the Heavenly Court, the judges were about to issue a harsh judgment against him because of his aggression towards a great Tzadik and the suffering he caused him. However, a defending angel then rose and pointed out the rich man's large number of good deeds, his accomplishments in Torah study, and how he had even generously supported the Rebbe and his household for many years.

Other angels joined in, pro and con. Finally it was decreed that he would be given the chance to appease Rabbi Nachum.

If he succeeded in gaining the Tzadik's forgiveness, he would be granted the rewards for the many good deeds he had accomplished in his lifetime.

He was assigned to two angels who would escort him to R. Nachum, and subsequently bring him back to the Heavenly Court.

The rich man's soul came to the Chernobyler and begged forgiveness for all the pain and aggravation he had caused him. The Rebbe told him to enumerate each of the offenses he had committed. At each one, the Tzadik responded, "I forgive him with all my heart."

Finally, they reached the episode with Rabbi Nachum's daughter. "No!" exclaimed the Rebbe adamantly, "This I may not forgive. This was a crime against my holy ancestors and against Heaven, not just against my daughter and me."

Immediately, the escorting angels took him and returned to the Heavenly Court, where a second decree was issued. He would be reincarnated, and in his next lifetime, would suffer from terrible physical afflictions.

After the Chernobyler passed away and his son Rabbi Mordechai succeeded him, Rabbi Nachum appeared to his son in a dream and asked him to take the young man with the skin diseases into his house. Rabbi Motteleh did so. He did nothing to ease the man's afflictions. He refrained from offering to help, because he knew it was atonement for the sins of his previous life. Finally, however, constantly confronted with how much the servant was suffering, the Rebbe could no longer hold back. He forgave the man for abusing his family. His spiritual rectification completed, the man's soul returned to heaven.

Source: Translated and freely adapted by Yerachmiel Tilles from *Niflaos HaTsaddikim*. (First published in *Kfar Chabad Magazine* #776.)

Double Treatment 11

Biographical notes for this story:

Rabbi **Elimelech of Lizensk** [of blessed memory: 5477– 21 Adar 5547 (1717– March 1787 C.E.)], was a leading disciple of the Maggid of Mezritch, successor to the Baal Shem Tov, and the leading Rebbe of the subsequent generation in Poland-Galitzia. Most of the great chasidic dynasties stem from his disciples. His book, Noam Elimelech, is one of the most popular of all chasidic works.

18th Century Eastern Europe

Rabbi **Zusha of Anapoli** [of blessed memory: ?– 2 Shvat 5560 (?– Jan. 1800 C.E.)], was also a major disciple of the Maggid. The seemingly unsophisticated but clearly inspired Reb Zushya is one of the best known and most beloved chasidic personalities. He and his famous brother, the Rebbe Elimelech of Lizensk, spent many years wandering in exile, for esoteric reasons.

This story can be related to:

Weekly Readings: *Beshalach* — Exodus 15:26 ("...I, G-d, am your healer.")

The Jewish Holidays: Rosh Hodesh *Iyar* ("Iyar" is also an acrostic of the initial letters of the above quote!)

Jewish Calendar Date: *Adar-a* 21 (week after Purim in a non leap-year on the Jewish calendar) — *yahrzeit* of the Rebbe Elimelech of Lizensk; *Shvat* 2 (two weeks before Tu b'Shvat) — *yahrzeit* of Rebbe Zushya of Anipoli.

Main Themes: Torah study, Healing

Other Topics: Divine inspiration, Becoming a chasid, Mothers

Double Treatment

THE GREAT TORAH SCHOLAR, Rabbi **Simcha of Bubraka** (cited in *Pri Magadim*), once fell critically sick. As he was not at all a believer in chasidic rebbes, his mother went without his knowledge to the famous holy Rebbe, Rabbi **Elimelech of Lizensk**, to request his blessing for her son's recovery. He told her not to be afraid, and with G-d's help, her son would regain his full health.

He told her that when she arrived home, she would find her son even weaker than he was before. Shortly thereafter, the lord of the area would host a gala affair, to which three great doctors from the big city of Lvov would be invited. She was to request that these three examine her ailing son. When they would come to her home, they would see how extremely weak her son was and would despair of his life. Nevertheless, she should not lose hope.

After they would leave the house, the Rebbe Elimelech continued, one of the three doctors would fall down while they were walking through the market place. His companions would help him stand up, and at that moment one of them would suddenly remember a certain medicine which would be able to help the sick Torah scholar.

This doctor would return to her home and write a prescription for that medicine. When she administered that medicine to her son, his condition would immediately begin to improve and eventually he would regain his full strength. The *Tzadik* concluded his words by instructing her that as soon as her son was healthy, he should travel to the Tzadik Rabbi **Zushya of Anapoli**, brother of the Rebbe Elimelech.

The woman returned home, and all the events that the holy Rebbe had foretold came to be, to the last detail. When the scholar was cured his mother related to him all that had happened. The son was very moved, and said that before he would travel to Anapoli, he and his mother must go to Lizensk to thank the Rebbe Elimelech in person.

Shortly thereafter they went. As soon as the Rebbe Elimelech laid eyes on them, he asked if they had fulfilled his instructions to go to see his brother. They responded that Anapoli was a great distance away and the recovered invalid was not yet strong enough for that.

A short while after, Rabbi Simcha travelled to Anapoli. There, a man came up to him in the street and said, "Simcha! I still don't have a guest for Shabbos. So you shall be my guest for the holy day."

The scholar was astonished. How did this man know the first name of a stranger from a distant city? Seeing a teenage boy walking nearby, the scholar asked him the identity of the man walking ahead of them. "That's our Rebbe," the boy said. The scholar was happy and excited that he had encountered R. Zushya so quickly, and went along with him to his home.

When they arrived, the Rebbe turned to him and said, "Simcha! Did you review the weekly Torah reading yet? No? Then take a *Chumash* [Five Books of Moses], and go over it now."

Afterwards, the Rebbe told him to come with him to the *mikveh*, and cautioned him to immerse while he, Zushya, was still in the water. The scholar carefully followed all the instructions. After they came out and got dressed, Reb Zushya asked him, "Simcha, do you have any difficulties in your studies?"

When Rabbi Simcha got back to his hotel, he thrust himself into his studies and reviewed all the thorny problems he had come up with in the Talmud and the Early Authorities, which even after all the time he had put into them, still seemed almost unsolvable. Now, he suddenly found all those difficulties to be easily resolved and was left with hardly a question unsolved.

Needless to say, the famed scholar, Rabbi Simcha of Bubraka, became a devoted follower of the Rebbe Reb Zushya of Anapoli.

Source: Translated by Yerachmiel Tilles from *Sipurei Chasidim-Torah* #447 — ***not*** included in Artscroll's English version! — by Rabbi S. Y. Zevin. (First published on *AscentOf Safed. com.*)

12 Beginner's Luck

Biographical note for this story:

Rabbi **Levi Yitzchak** (Deberamdiger) **of Berditchev** [of blessed memory: 5500– 25 Tishrei 5571 (1740– Oct. 1810 C.E.)] is one of the more popular rebbes in chasidic history. He was a close disciple of the second leader of the chasidic movement, Rabbi DovBer, the *Maggid of Mezritch*, successor to the *Baal Shem Tov*. He is best known for his love for every Jew and his perpetual intercession before Heaven on their behalf. Many of his teachings are contained in the posthumously published *Kedushat Levi*.

12
18th Century (2nd half) Eastern Europe

This story can be related to:

Weekly Readings: *Shoftim* — Deuteronomy 16:18–20 ("Appoint yourselves judges ... in all your cities ... They shall not pervert justice; nor show favoritism ... Justice, justice shall you pursue....")

Jewish Calendar Date: *Tishrei* 25 (a few days after Simchat Torah) — *yahrzeit* of the Berditchever Rebbe.

Main Themes: Rabbinical court, Orphans

Other Topics: Judges, Buying and selling, Divine justice

Beginner's Luck

LESS THAN A WEEK after the Tzadik Rabbi **Levi Yitzchak** moved to Berdichev in 5745 (1785 C.E.) to serve as chief rabbi there, three men knocked on his door to ask him to judge a question of Jewish law for them. It would be his very first case as a rabbinical judge in his new position.

A wealthy merchant from the nearby town of Hemelnick had brought several barrels filled with honey to sell at the big fair in Berdichev. Unfortunately, just then, the price of honey dropped sharply. Not wanting to suffer a loss on his investment, he asked an acquaintance to store the honey for him until the price would rise again.

The two were old friends, and the local man was happy to oblige. Knowing each other to be completely honest, they didn't write down anything of their arrangement or call in witnesses.

Time went by. The price of honey remained low, so the barrels remained in their Berdichev cellar, untouched and unnoticed.

More time went by. The man on whose property the honey was stored contracted a fatal disease and passed away. Everything happened so quickly that he never had a chance to explain to his family anything about the state of his affairs.

More time passed. The price of honey finally began to slowly climb. When the increase became significant, the owner of the barrels showed up at his deceased friend's house and claimed his honey from the sons who had inherited and taken over their father's business. They, however, having heard nothing about it from their father, refused to honor the Hemelnicker merchant's claim. After some discussion, they decided to proceed to the *bet-din* (rabbinical court) to present the case before the new rabbi.

Rabbi Levi Yitzchak listened to the litigants carefully, even though the law in such a case was clear. Of course he would have to rule against the out-of-town merchant. Even if there had been witnesses or a signed document, Torah law stipulates that claims against "orphans" (i.e., heirs who are disadvantaged by the fact that they have no way of knowing what transpired between the deceased and their litigant) cannot be collected without first swearing an oath as to the validity of one's claim; and here there were neither documents nor witnesses.

Nevertheless, Rabbi Levi Yitzchak hesitated to pronounce his verdict and resolve the case. Two nagging thoughts disturbed him. Why, in his first days in his new position, did the Almighty arrange for his inaugural judgment to be something so straightforward and clear-cut, with no room to maneuver left or right to attempt to arrive at any sort of compromise? Could it be a hint from Heaven that his practice to always pursue accommodation and compromise was not correct? That only adhering strictly to the letter of the law can be considered the way of truth?

The other thought that made him uncomfortable, perhaps even more than the first, was: Why did the Supernal Judge arrange it so that his very first ruling in this town would be considered bizarre by the entire populace? After all, the merchant from Hemelnick was well-known to everyone in town as a scrupulously honest man, as someone who was already wealthy and as such immune to monetary pressure, and as far from theft as east is from west. Furthermore, everyone knew that the merchant and the deceased were old friends who trusted each other explicitly, never resorting to documents or witnesses in their transactions.

Surely, the entire town would be paying attention to the first ruling handed down by their new rabbi. Everyone was sure to wonder: Why should the law of the Torah be so opposite to common sense? "Why me and why now?" thought Rabbi Levi Yitzchak to himself.

He couldn't bring himself to issue the verdict just yet. The contradiction between the natural sense of what was right and the law of the Torah was too great. Even though the claimant and defendants anxiously awaited his decision, he asked them to excuse him for a few more minutes.

Turning aside to a corner of the room, he poured forth in silent prayer his frustration, beseeching G-d to enlighten him with understanding.

Suddenly, the owner of the honey jumped off his seat as if struck by a bolt of lightning, and exclaimed: "I remember! I remember!" So struck was he by his recollection, and so convinced of its importance and relevance, that he didn't hesitate to interrupt the rabbi, who was standing in the corner, absorbed in his personal prayer.

"Honored Rabbi, please forgive me," he called out excitedly. "While waiting here I had the most amazing realization! An old memory, which I haven't thought about in many years, just flashed through my mind. Rescued from oblivion! I'm talking about something that happened fifty-three years ago, when I was just a lad of 14.

"Our father died suddenly, leaving us a large inheritance in cash and possessions. Included in this was a storage room filled with casks of wine and oil.

"One day, the grandfather of these two young men, may his rest be peaceful, came to our home in Hemelnick. He claimed that the wine and oil were his, that he had stored them with our father for safekeeping. My brothers and I were still quite young then, and had never been involved in any of our father's business affairs. We had no idea what we were supposed to do, but we were reluctant to give up the merchandise just like that.

"We all went to the rabbi of the town and presented our case. He ruled in our favor, explaining that nothing can be taken from the inheritance of orphans without absolute proof and an oath. The wine and oil remained in our possession. After a while, we sold the entire lot for a good price.

"What I just realized is that the money we received for that wine and oil is exactly equal to the value of my honey, which is now in the possession of the sons of my departed friend!"

Rabbi Levi Yitzchak's face shone with inner happiness. With his apt comparison of the two parallel events fifty plus years apart, the merchant had conceded his own present case. For the same reason that, as an orphan, he was entitled to keep the wine and oil from before, he had to relinquish his claim on these orphans for his honey that day.

Now, all was clear to Rabbi Levi Yitzchak. Divine Providence had presented him this case so early in his new tenure, to teach him an important lesson. What seems obvious and true to human eyes is not necessarily the truth, or even fair. Absolute truth resides only with the laws of the Torah. G-d's ledger is always open, and all accounts are forever being reckoned and balanced. Some may take fifty years for resolution, some more, and others less. What is guaranteed is that the Master of the Universe constantly oversees all to be sure that justice is done.

Source: Translated-adapted by Yerachmiel Tilles from the Hebrew weekly *Sichat HaShavua*, #593 and #1170. (First published on *chabad.org*, in 5762/2002.)

Special Delivery 13

Biographical note for this story:

Rabbi **Shneur Zalman** [of blessed memory: 18 Elul 5505– 24 Tevet 5573 (1745– Dec. 1812 C.E.)], one of the main disciples of the *Maggid of Mezritch*, is the founder — the "*Alter Rebbe*" — of the *Chabad* chasidic movement. He is the author of *Shulchan Aruch HaRav* and *Tanya* as well as many other major works in both Jewish law and the mystical teachings.

This story can be related to:

13

18th–19th Century Eastern Europe

Weekly Readings: *Vayeitzei* — Genesis 29:2 ("Yaakov lifted his feet and went..." — Rashi: "Because of the good news his heart lifted his feet and it was easy to go."); *Vayigash* — Genesis 45:26–28 ("They told him, 'Yosef is still alive' ... and the spirit of their father Yaakov revived.")

Jewish Calendar Date: *Tishrei* 13 (2 days before Sukkot) — *yahrzeit* of Rabbi Akiva Eiger; *Tevet* 24 (3 weeks after end of Chanukah) — *yahrzeit* of Rabbi Shneur Zalman.

Main Themes: Rebbe, Chasid, Thanksgiving

Other Topics: Deeds of kindness, Wealth and poverty, Israel, Tzefat

Special Delivery

Once, in a certain Russian town, a group of chasidim of the first Rebbe of Chabad, Rabbi **Shneur Zalman**, were being severely oppressed because of their chasidic practices. Some of the chasidim were even arrested, and jailed due to the slander and false accusations presented to the local authorities. G-d was merciful, however, and the innocent victims were released. They immediately sat down together to write a letter to the Rebbe, informing him of the good news of their deliverance.

Among this group was a poor tinsmith named Shimon. He was only average in his ability to study and comprehend the texts of Talmud and of chasidic philosophy, but he was strongly bonded to the Rebbe with love and dedication. Often, he was heard to spontaneously cry out, "Oy Rebbe!" This Shimon took it upon himself to arrange the delivery of the letter to the Rebbe. Instead of sending it by regular mail, he decided to hire a private messenger in order that their letter get to the Rebbe absolutely as soon as possible. He arranged to pay for the extra costs out of his own pocket.

In those days, every Chabad (chasidic) community had its own council, which would supervise all communal matters. The council members were all well-acquainted with Shimon's dire economic situation — how he sometimes had to trek from village to village to find more work, how he barely managed to support his family at the most minimal level, and how his wife and children were sick. When he said he intended to pay the expensive fees for the express messenger out of his own meager funds, they refused to hear it. They told him he shouldn't do it.

Shimon, however, refused to accept their decision. He said that the good news of their release would give the Rebbe relief and happiness, and if such news could reach the Rebbe even just one hour earlier, it was worth more to him then all the wealth in the world.

As part of the council, one chasidic elder in each community was responsible for matters of education and guidance, and he would report on a regular basis directly to the Rebbe. When the matter of the messenger was brought before the elder chasid in this position in Shimon's town, who also oversaw the fundraising campaigns for the Rabbi Meir Baal HaNess fund [to support the fledgling chasidic community in the Holy Land, mostly in Tzefat and Tiberias] and for "*Maimad*" [to support the Rebbe's household], he countered the council's advice and endorsed the tinsmith's choice.

Eventually, the report of what Shimon had done became known to the "*Maharil*" (Rabbi Yehuda Leib, brother of Rabbi Shneur Zalman), who had been appointed by the Rebbe to be the overall supervisor in Chabad communal matters of *tsedakah*, and he mentioned it to his brother, the Rebbe.

After some time had passed, one of the leading chasidim, Rabbi Yaakov of Semillian, arrived in the town as an emissary of the Rebbe. He had been sent to collect money for the above-mentioned campaigns from all the chasidic communities in that area of Russia. Much to the astonishment of the chasidim, who had all gathered to meet with him, he delivered a letter to Reb Shimon the tinsmith, which was written in the personal handwriting of the Rebbe! In it the Rebbe thanked him for arranging a special messenger to deliver the good tidings of the release. The Rebbe concluded by blessing R. Shimon that G-d Al-mighty should bless him to always be a bearer of good news.

Not long after that, R. Shimon's situation started to improve. His wife and children became healthy, and he himself began to prosper greatly. The Rebbe's blessing was fulfilled. Because R. Shimon the tinsmith exerted himself to make another Jew happy, and especially a great tzadik, and at great personal sacrifice, he merited to become a bearer of happy news for himself and his family, and of the chasidim of his town.

Source: Translated and freely adapted by Yerachmiel Tilles from "*Ahavat Yisrael*" #2. (An earlier, shorter version was published in *Kfar Chabad Magazine-English* #791.)

Crossroad Puzzle 14

Biographical note for this story:

R. **Yaakov Yitzchok Horowitz** [of blessed memory: 5505– 9 Av 5575 (1745– Aug. 1815 C.E.)], known as 'the ***Chozeh*** **(Seer) of Lublin**', was the successor to the Rebbe Elimelech of Lizensk (see the bio note for story #11), and presided over the spread of Chasidut in Poland. Many of his insights were published posthumously in *Divrei Emmes, Zichron Zos,* and *Zos Zichron.*

This story can be related to:

Jewish Calendar Date: 9 Av (Tisha B'Av) — yahrzeit of the Chozeh.

Main Themes: Hospitality, Divine supervision

Other Topics: Education, Burial

14
18th Century (end) Eastern Europe

Crossroad Puzzle

One Friday, the famed chasidic master known as the **Seer of Lublin** was traveling with some of his disciples when they arrived at a crossroads. The wagon driver asked which way to turn. Surprisingly, the Seer didn't seem to know what to answer. Shrugging, he said, "Loosen the reins. Let the horses go in whichever direction they will."

After a while, they arrived at a town. After several enquiries, they soon realized that not only was this not the place they were seeking, but they were not even on the right road.

"It's late. We'll stay here for Shabbat," the Seer announced. Then he added, "But don't reveal my identity to anyone or tell them that I am a Rebbe."

His followers were shocked. They had no money because the Seer never allowed any to be kept overnight; however much one had in his possession would be distributed to poor people before nightfall. If his identity as a great tzadik were to be kept secret, perhaps no one would offer them Shabbat hospitality.

When they asked him, he replied, "We'll do like all Jewish travelers. We'll go to the local shul tonight, and people will invite us when they see we have no place to go."

And so they did. They prayed at the back of the shul, and afterwards, all of the Rebbe's students and attendants were invited individually to different homes. The Seer, however, was left in the shul. He always took a long time for the Shabbat evening prayers and this week was no exception. By the time he finished, almost everyone was gone.

In fact, there was just one other person in the shul, an old man at least eighty years old. He saw that the stranger was sitting and reciting "*Tikunei Shabbat*" (selected passages usually recited during the course of the meal on Friday night).

"Where are you going for your Shabbat meal?" he asked the Seer.

"I don't know."

"Why don't you eat at the inn where you are staying?" questioned the elderly man, concerned. "If it is a problem of money, after Shabbat I'll collect some money to pay your bill."

"I saw they didn't light Shabbat candles, so I presume that I cannot trust that the food they serve there is kosher."

"I'm sorry," murmured the older man, "but at my house my wife and I will have only bread and wine."

"I'm neither a glutton nor a guzzler."*

"Come along then," said the apprehensive host. The Seer followed meekly.

After *kiddush* and *hamotzei* [blessings upon the wine and bread at the beginning of a festive meal], while they were sitting calmly at the table, the elderly man asked him where he was from. Upon hearing his answer, he next asked him if he knew the Rebbe of Lublin.

"I am always with him," was the Seer's reply.

"That's wonderful," said his host. "Please tell me something about him."

"Why do you want to know about him?" queried the Seer in response.

"Because," said the man, "I was his teacher in *cheder* [(Jewish school for young boys] when he was a small boy, and he was not noticeably exceptional in his studies. Now I hear that he is a great rabbi and does miracles."

"Did you notice anything unusual about him when he was a child?" the Seer asked.

"Only one thing," the retired teacher replied. "Each morning, when I would want to call upon him to read from the siddur, I could never find him. He vanished! Later, when he would re-appear, I would punish him for his unauthorized absence. "One day, I decided, 'Enough already! I ought to find out where he disappears to.' I watched him closely out of the corner of my eye. When he exited the room I slipped out after him, keeping a good distance between us so he wouldn't sense my presence.

"I followed him into the forest and peered through the trees. There he was, sitting next to a hive, being stung, and crying out, '*Shma Yisrael! Ad-ny Elokeinu Ad-ny echad*' ('Hear O Israel: the L-rd our G-d, the L-rd is one' — Judaism's most basic prayer).

"After that, I never punished him again. Now, after all these years, I would very much like to be able to see him in his glory, but I don't know how it can be. I'm very poor and I've become weak in my old age, so it is impossible for me to make the journey to Lublin. Nevertheless, my desire is so strong, I fast one day a week that I should have the merit to see him with my own eyes."

Finally, the Seer understood why events had been directed to bring him to this particular town. Looking fondly at his host, he acknowledged gently, "I am he, the Rebbe of Lublin."

The old man fainted instantly. His wife and special guest were able to revive him only after great difficulty.

That Saturday night the Seer and his entourage departed the town and continued their journey. The elderly man escorted them briefly and then returned home. They stopped at the Seer's request at a not-too-distant village, in order to enjoy *Melaveh Malka* (the special meal of Saturday night).

After the meal, the Seer said, "Now let us return to that town to attend my childhood teacher's funeral and to deliver an appropriate eulogy."

Source: *Shemu Vitachi Nafshechem* (#266), featuring teachings and stories of Rabbi Moshe Weber (story #32 in this book). (First published in *Kfar Chabad Magazine* #825.)]

End note:

—

* (See Deuteronomy 21:20)

Translator's notes:

—

I hope everyone realizes that this is a happy story, not a sad one.

15 What You See is What You Get

Biographical notes for this story:

Rabbi **Avraham Yehoshua Heschel** [of blessed memory: 5515– 5 Nissan 5585 (1755– March 1825 C.E.)], the **Apter Rebbe**, was a main disciple of the Rebbe Elimelech of Lizhinsk. He is also often referred to as the *Ohev Yisrael*, both after the title of the famous book of his teachings, and also because its meaning, *Lover of Jews*, fits him so aptly.

This story can be related to:

Weekly Readings: *Netzavim* — Deuteronomy 29:26 ("The secret things are for GD, our Gd, while the revealed belongs to us and our children."); *Pirkei Avot* 1:6 ("...Judge every person favorably." — studied on the first Shabbat after Passover)

Jewish Calendar Date: *Nissan* 5 (ten days before Passover) — *yahrzeit* of the Apter Rebbe.

Main Themes: Divine inspiration

Other Topics: Prayer, Reincarnation, Seer of Lublin

What You See is What You Get

RABBI AHARON-MOSHE was a follower of Rabbi **Yaakov Yitzchok Horowitz**, the Seer of Lublin. He always made an effort to spend as little time as possible in the company of Jewish sinners. This was not because he looked down upon them, or even that he did not have feelings of love for them as his fellow-Jews. Neither was the case.

Rather, his level of purity was such that with one glance his penetrating spiritual vision could detect their most intimate secrets, including every physical sin they had done. This awareness made him so uncomfortable that he avoided such encounters whenever he possibly could.

One time he happened to be in the same place as Rabbi **Avraham-Yehoshua Heschel**, the Rebbe of Apt, known to one and all as the *Ohev Yisrael* (Lover of Jews). The chasid seized the opportunity to consult with him, and asked, plaintively, "What shall I do if I am able to see into the hearts of others and what I see distresses me so?"

The Rebbe (who often referred to himself in the plural) replied, "My dear Aharon-Moshe, in our youth we also saw things. When a Jew would come before us, we would immediately know what he was and what his deeds were, how many incarnations he had been through, and what his mistakes and blemishes were in each lifetime.

"Later on, we came to the realization that it is not appropriate to see into another Jew's heart and the mysteries that are concealed there, in order to perceive things that are not positive. So we prayed to the Merciful One that He remove from us this ability. Since then, whenever a Jew comes before us, we see only the good deeds and the soul-rectifications that he accomplished in each incarnation.

"So you, too, Aharon-Moshe, should request this of the Al-mighty, and thereby cease to perceive what is not necessary to see."

"The secret things are for G-D, our G-d, while the revealed belongs to us and our children." [Deuteronomy 29:28]

Source: Translated-adapted by Yerachmiel Tilles from the Hebrew weekly *Sichat HaShavua*, #1073. (First published on *AscentOfSafed.com*.)

The Joker's Shabbat 16

Biographical notes for this story:

Rabbi **Chaim Tirar of Czernowitz** [of blessed memory: 5520– 27 Kislev 5577 (1760– December 1817 C.E.)] was a leading disciple of the *Maggid of Mezritch*, successor to the *Baal Shem Tov*, and of Rabbi Yechiel Michel of Zlotchov, another main student of the *Baal Shem Tov*. He authored a number of important books, including *Siduro Shel Shabbat*, which explains the exaltedness and holiness of the Seventh Day according to mystical principles of kabbalah. However, he is best known for, and by, the name of his esoteric commentary on the Torah, *Be'er Mayim Chaim*. Towards the end of his life he moved to Tzefat (Safed), where he is buried.

This story can be related to:

16

19th Century (1st half)
Eastern Europe

Weekly Readings: *Yitro* — Exodus 20:8 ("Remember the Shabbat Day for it to be holy."); *Ki Tisa* — Exodus 31:16–17 ("It [Shabbat] is a sign between Me and the Children of Israel for all times....")

The Jewish Holidays: *Chanukah, Shavuot*

Jewish Calendar Date: *Kislev* 27 3rd day of *Chanukah*) — *yahrzeit* of the *Be'er Mayim Chayim*

Main Themes: Shabbat, Deeds of kindness

Other Topics: Redeeming captives, Chasid-Rebbe, Tzefat.

The Joker's Shabbat

HERSHEL DIDN'T JUST tell jokes, he breathed them. Certainly it seemed to the people in his village of Mosayov in the Marmorash area that he had never drawn a serious breath in his life. He lived for laughs. Nothing was too sacred or out of bounds to be the target of his rough humor. Fear of G-d? The very notion was laughable to him. The grin never left Hershel's face.

As might be expected, Hershel soon became the most popular guy in Mosayov among the idle, the crude, the silly and the drinkers. Whenever there was a crowd of people on the street or in the village tavern laughing hilariously, one was sure to find Hershel at the epicenter, perfecting his craft.

Hershel himself was not among the unemployed. He made a nice living as a seller of livestock. As his business took him to all the neighboring towns and villages, his reputation as a comedian spread throughout the Marmorash region.

Each year Hershel would travel to the annual great livestock fair in Czernowitz. Another person who consistently attended the fair was the rabbi of the city, the well-known tzadik and scholarly author, Rabbi **Chaim of Czernowitz**. Rabbi Chaim would circulate among the merchants and accord them the opportunity to contribute to the many worthy causes that he was involved in for helping needy people and educational institutions.

One day during the week of the fair, as Rabbi Chaim was making his rounds of the stalls, he came across a large group of fairgoers laughing raucously, slapping their thighs and winking at each other. No doubt about it, Hershel the Mosayover had to be in the midst of them, and in top form, too.

Rabbi Chaim thought to slip around them inconspicuously. He knew that from these crude, empty-headed types he could not expect much 'business' anyway, but Hershel was quicker than he. "Hey! Holy Rebbe! *Shalom aleichem,*" he called out, still grinning from the last joke he had successfully cracked.

"*Aleichem shalom*, my fellow Jews," responded the rabbi warmly. The die was cast. He could no longer turn away. "Perhaps you gentlemen would care to take a share in the great *mitzvah* of charity?"

"And what, exactly, is this charity for?" asked Hershel, still smirking.

"For *pidyon shavuyim* (redeeming captive Jews), called the greatest mitzvah of all," the rabbi responded promptly. "There is a poor, unfortunate Jew who has a large debt of 1,500 *zlotys* (Polish gold currency) to his local *poritz* (noble landowner). Now he is languishing in the nobleman's dungeon until the debt is paid."

Hershel's companions were all grinning in anticipation. They waited eagerly for their friend's witty riposte in the rabbi-jester dialogue.

Hershel put his hand in his pocket and took out 1,500 *zalatys*, all the money he had brought with him to replenish his livestock. "Here you are, Rabbi," he said quietly, with a strange look on his face. "Here is the entire sum you need to ransom that unfortunate Jew."

All the onlookers were startled for a moment, but then they realized this must be one of Hershel's clever jests. The naïve rabbi would put out his hand for the money, and Hershel would pretend to start to give it to him, and then at the last moment he would snatch it back, making a fool of the gullible Torah scholar.

But the tzadik was not so naive after all. He held back, and simply gazed at the well-known clown thoughtfully.

"No, no," exclaimed Hershel, as his face took on a fully

serious expression. "I really mean it. No joke. Please. Take the money." As he spoke the words, he approached the rabbi and pressed the bulging wallet he had drawn out of his pocket into Rabbi Chaim's hand.

The astonished rabbi felt himself overwhelmed with emotion — excitement and relief at being able to secure the release of the poor imprisoned Jew, and amazement that such a lowly soul could ascend to the highest of peaks in the briefest of moments. His cheeks were flushed; warm tears pooled at the corner of his eyes.

Hershel himself was stunned. He couldn't understand what he had just done. It had been a spontaneous impulse that had overcome him, but why had it been so irresistible?

The tzadik wished to bless his donor appropriately, but wasn't sure how. For Rabbi Chaim, life turned on one hinge: Shabbat. He had even written a unique book, *Siduro Shel Shabbat*, explaining the exaltedness and holiness of the Seventh Day according to mystical principles of Kabblah, but how was that relevant to the loutish man that stood before him? Nevertheless, he thought to himself, such a deed deserves the greatest blessing of all. Still brimming with enthusiasm, he exclaimed,

"I bless you that, in the merit of this great mitzvah that you have done, you will experience the true taste of Shabbat."

Hershel was still numb. He nodded his head as if he understood what the tzadik was talking about, and answered, "Amen."

That very day Hershel returned to Mosayov. Since he had no money, there was no reason to remain in Czernowitz. Still, he remained his cheerful, joking self.

As the week progressed, however, he began to feel a strange feeling welling up inside him, a spiritual pulling, something he had never felt before in his life. When Friday dawned and the feeling was even more intense, he realized that it must be connected to the oncoming Shabbat, and that this Shabbat would definitely be like no other he had ever experienced.

He went shopping to purchase the special foods for Shabbat, and he could barely control his trembling. As the hours went by his inner upheaval grew stronger and stronger. He couldn't imagine what would happen when Shabbat actually arrived.

All those who encountered Hershel that Shabbat could hardly recognize him. Was that really him singing, dancing, studying, and praying with ecstasy? Hershel could barely recognize himself! His entire being was bursting with the sacred pleasure of Shabbat.

It was the talk of the town. The idea that Hershel the clown could be caught up in a tzadik-type of intense love of Shabbat cracked up everyone who heard it even more than Hershel's intentional jests. They even entertained the possibility that he had gone insane.

Then the news spread about what had happened at the livestock fair in Czernowitz — the incongruous charitable deed that Hershel had done and the extraordinary blessing of the Tzadik of Czernowitz. Then people began to consider the issue more seriously.

After that Shabbat, Hershel returned to his customary light-hearted joking manner, but by the following Shabbat he was again overwhelmed by the same spirit of holiness. It was as if there were two Hershels: the weekday persona and the special Shabbat one.

Weeks went by, then months, without a change in his situation. Hershel felt himself cracking under the strain of his dual personality. He decided to travel back to Czernowitz to discuss his situation with the *tzadi*k who had blessed him.

Rabbi Chaim told him that in order to absorb the taste of Shabbat without spiritual and psychological damage, he would have to refine his weekday behavior. Hershel decided to stay on in Czernowitz in order to learn more from his new mentor. Soon his daily lifestyle slowly but steadily evolved to be harmonious with his weekly Shabbat elevation. Frivolous

Hershel had become a completely different person!

In the early 1800's, Rabbi Chaim of Czernovitz moved to the Land of Israel and his faithful disciple Hershel accompanied him. They lived in the holy city of Tzefat. Today, nearly two centuries later, their burial sites are well known and frequently visited.

Source: Translated-adapted by Yerachmiel Tilles from the Hebrew weekly *Sichat HaShavua*, #461. (First published on *AscentOfSafed.com*.)

PART III

Chasidic Masters: The 2nd hundred years 1820–1920 (C.E.)

Forty Days and Forty Nights

Biographical notes:

Rabbi **Yisrael Friedmann of Rhyzhin** [1797– 3 Cheshvan 1850 C.E.] was a great-grandson of the *Maggid of Mezritch*, successor to the *Baal Shem Tov*. At a young age, he was already a charismatic leader with a large following of chasidim. Greatly respected by the other rebbes and Jewish leaders of his generation, he was, and still is, referred to as *The Holy Rhyzhiner*. Six of his sons established chasidic dynasties, several of which, *Sadigora, Chortkov*, etc., are still thriving today.

This story can be related to:

Weekly Readings: *Noach* — Genesis 7:17 ("There was a flood on the earth for forty days.")

Jewish Calendar Date: *Cheshvan* 3 (around parshat *Noach*) — *yahrzeit* of the "holy Rhyzhiner"

Main Themes: Elijah the Prophet, Holiness

Other Topics: Torah study, Kabbalah, Wealth, Horses

Forty Days and Forty Nights

HE WAS A NOTED SCHOLAR who had accomplished much in his Torah study career. Now he had discovered in an obscure tome of Kabbalah that if a suitable person were to pass forty days and forty nights without uttering a single unnecessary word, he would merit the exalted spiritual state of *ruach hakodesh* (divine inspiration).

Excited, he decided to attempt it. He spent as much time as he could studying Torah, and avoided social contact as much as he could. The required time period passed without a mishap, and he exhaled deeply in relief, but then he became short of breath again, as he began to tremble in anticipation of the blessed revelation.

After the evening prayer, he isolated himself in his room and waited and waited, and waited.

He couldn't understand. What had gone wrong? He knew with certainty that he hadn't failed the requirement. Perhaps he had miscounted the days?

But another day and night went by, and another, and another, and still the blessed bestowal did not happen. How could this possibly be?

He decided to journey and consult the chasidic rebbe he had heard so much about, Rabbi **Yisrael of Rhyzhin.**

When he arrived at the Rebbe's court, he was astonished at what he saw. The Rebbe lived in extraordinary luxury! Home, furnishings, clothing and appurtenances were all made of the most expensive materials and were of a quality fit for the highest level of aristocratic decadence. Was this any way for a spiritual leader to live, and a chasidic rebbe no less?

He wondered if he had made a mistake in coming there, and as the days passed he became convinced he had. How could a person who lived in such opulent style possibly have anything to tell him about divine inspiration? He decided to leave for home without even speaking to the so-called holy master.

As he passed by the Rhyzhiner's house, he saw the Rebbe emerge. Four magnificent white steeds had been harnessed to a carriage worthy of royalty. As the Rebbe was about to mount to his seat, he paused, and then patted one of the horses on the head, three times.

This was too much for the frustrated scholar to bear. He dashed over to the Rebbe and challenged, "Explain to me, please, exalted sir, what spiritual work is a chasidic master engaged in during the time he is petting a horse?"

The Rhyzhiner gazed at him a moment before answering benignly, "Ah, but you do not understand. This special horse just completed forty days and nights without uttering a single unnecessary word!"

Source: Translated and freely adapted by Yerachmiel Tilles from *Sipurei Chasidim-Torah* (# 147) by Rabbi S. Y. Zevin. (First published on *AscentOfSafed.com*.)

Translator's note:

—

A variant of this story has the man consulting the *Baal Shem Tov*, who asks him, "During the forty days and nights, did you pray all the daily prayers? Did you recite Psalms?"

18 Yaakov the Innocent

Biographical notes for this story:

Rabbi **Menachem Mendel Schneersohn,** [29 Elul 1789– 13 Nissan 1866 C.E.], the third Rebbe of Chabad, was known as the ***Tzemach Tzedek***, after his books of Jewish Law responsa and Talmudic commentary called by that name. He was renowned not only as a Rebbe, but also as a leading scholar in his generation in both the revealed and hidden aspects of Torah.

Rabbi **Yisrael Friedmann of Rhyzhin** [1797– 3 Cheshvan 1850 C.E.] was a great-grandson of the *Maggid of Mezritch*, successor to the *Baal Shem Tov*. At a young age he was already a charismatic leader with a large following of chasidim. Greatly respected by the other rebbes and Jewish leaders of his generation, he was — and still is — referred to as "*The Holy Rhyzhiner*." Six of his sons established chasidic dynasties, several of which, *Sadigora, Chortkov,* etc, are still thriving today.

18

19th Century (1st half) Eastern Europe

This story can be related to:

Weekly Readings: *Mishpatim* — Exodus 22:24 ("...the poor person among you, do not press him for repayment..."); *Bahar* — Leviticus 25:35 ("When your brother becomes impoverished and his hand is inadequate with you, you must come to his aid ... he shall live with you."); *Re'ey* — Deuteronomy 13:7–8 ("...Do not harden your heart against your needy brother; ...extend to him credit for his lacks").

Jewish Calendar Date: *Nissan* 13 (2 days before Passover) — *yahrzeit* of the *Tzemach Tzedek*.

Main Themes: Afterlife

Other Topics: Landlord, Debts, Deeds of kindness, Heavenly Court, Chasid-Rebbe, Innocence

Yaakov the Innocent

As a result of a devastating fire, new houses had to be built for the ***Tsemech Tzedek*** and his sons. The day the cornerstone was laid, a large number of chasidim attended the ceremony.

A table and chair were set up for the Rebbe at the construction site. He sat, and asked the chasidim which they would truly prefer for him to say for them: a chasidic discourse or a story? The surprised chasidim were quick to choose the story. They explained that lessons in chasidic themes we merit to hear from the Rebbe fairly often, but stories only rarely.

The Tsemech Tsedek acceded to their request, and told the following.

Ya'akov Ish Tam made his living by leasing the land and rights to all the business and agricultural properties belonging to a certain *poritz* (duke), and then sub-letting them to different individuals. He rented one inn to a certain Jew, who was unable to come up with the rent money he owed at the end of the year. Yaakov Ish-Tam sent notice to the man that he had better pay the money or else he would be forced to evict him.

It so happened that Yaakov Ish-Tam and the innkeeper were both chasidim of the famous Rebbe, Rabbi **Yisroel of Rhyzhin**. The desperate tenant traveled to the Rebbe and asked him to intercede with Yaakov Ish-Tam to ask him to wait another year, whereupon with Gd's help he would pay him for both years.

The tzadik was successful, and Yaakov Ish-Tam agreed to the delay. However, at the end of the second year, the poor man's situation had not improved at all and again he was unable to pay for either year.

Yaakov Ish-Tam told the man to go look for another place, because now he was two years in arrears. The poor lessee once again went to the Rhyzhiner Rebbe to ask him to intercede again, saying that surely G-d will help him, and at the end of the next year he will pay off the entire debt. Once again the Rebbe was able to influence Yaakov Ish-Tam to not pressure the innkeeper, and wait an additional year.

After the third year was up, there was still no money forthcoming. This time, the Rhyzhiner was unable to convince Yaakov Ish-Tam to wait a fourth year. The latter insisted he could not afford to give in to his Rebbe's appeal and proceeded with the eviction of the unfortunate tenant from the inn.

It was not long afterwards that Yaakov Ish-Tam returned his soul to his Maker. When his case came before the Heavenly Court, they found his record in the 613 *mitzvot* to be excellent, but there was still one serious charge against him. He had failed to heed a direct request of his Rebbe, the *Tzadik* of Rhyzhin.

The court ruled that he would have to enter *Gehinom* [Purgatory]. Suddenly, a man appeared and challenged the court's ruling. He pointed out how the members of the court were all souls that had been away from physical life for many, many years, and had forgotten or never knew how difficult monetary affairs in the flesh-and-blood world really are. That Yaakov Ish-Tam obeyed the Rhyzhiner twice and went without being paid the rent on the inn for three years was nothing short of extraordinary. To do so yet another time was simply beyond his strength and too much to expect.

"My opinion," concluded the Tsemech Tsedek, "is that Yaakov Ish-Tam is innocent*. What do you all think?"

Now the chasidim understood why the Rebbe had offered to tell a story. The Heavenly Court had agreed to use a judge and jury still in the world. The chasidim were quick to respond. "Innocent, innocent," they declared in unison.

Source: Translated-adapted by Yerachmiel Tilles from "*Rishimat Devorim*" by Rabbi Yehuda Chitrik, v.3, page 127–128, where it is recorded that this story was told by (the sixth Rabbi of Chabad,) Rabbi Yosef Yitzchak Schneersohn, in 1922, in Rostov. (First published in *Kfar Chabad Magazine* #767]

Translator's note:

—

* There is a layer of meaning that gets lost in translation here. The name, Ish-*tam*, can legitimately be translated as "innocent", although the sense is more the opposite of "sophisticated" or "complex" rather than the opposite of "guilty" — see Genesis 25:27 with *Rashi*.

The Onion Plot 19

Biographical notes for this story:

Rabbi **Naftali of Rofshitz** [of blessed memory: 6 Sivan 5520 (the same day as the *Baal Shem Tov*'s passing!) 11 Iyar 5587 (1760–1827 C.E.)] became the *rebbe* of many thousands of chasidim. He was noted for his sharp wit, humor, and his illuminating aphorisms. Some of his teachings are collected in his works, *Zera Kodesh, Ayalah Sheluchah,* and *Imrei Shefer.* Many stories about him appear in the book, *Ohel Naftoli.*

Rabbi **Yaakov Yitzchok Horowitz** [of blessed memory: 5505– 9 Av 5575 (1745– Aug. 1815 C.E.)], known as 'the ***Chozeh*** **(Seer) of Lublin**', was the successor to *R. Elimelech of Lizensk* (Lizensk (see the bio note for story #11), and leader of the spread of chasidism in Poland. Many of his insights were published posthumously in *Divrei Emmes, Zichron Zos,* and *Zos Zichron.*

This story can be related to:

Weekly Readings: *Beha'alotecha* — Numbers 11:5 ("We remember [fondly] ... that we could eat ... the onions....")

The Jewish Holidays: *Purim, Shavuot*

Jewish Calendar Date: *Iyar* 11 (4 weeks after Pesach) — *yahrzeit* of the Rofshitzer.

Main Themes: Shabbat, Disguises

Other Topics: Onions, Chasid-Rebbe, Non-Jews, Drunkenness, L'Chaim, Kiddush

The Onion Plot

Blizzards and storm winds had pounded Lublin and the surrounding countryside for several weeks. The roads were piled so high with snow that no one was able to go anywhere. This meant that the farmers weren't able to reach the city with their produce, and food supplies were dwindling rapidly.

Many items were completely lacking, such as onions. There weren't even any onions to use in the tasty foods prepared in honor of Shabbat. This fact constituted a near tragedy, because in Lublin, the mixture of chopped eggs and onions, known in Yiddish as *eiyr-un-tzibl*, was considered a nearly indispensable ingredient of the holy day. The Jews of Lublin could remember occasions when there was no meat, or no fish, but whoever heard of being without onions?

The household of the famous *Tzadik*, the **Seer of Lublin**, was particularly distraught. After all, chasidic tradition attaches great significance to this humble dish. They tried to secure some onions by every means they could think of, but to no avail. Someone even managed to plod his way through the snowdrifts to a few of the local farmers, but they didn't have any onions either.

On Friday morning, one of the leading disciples of the Seer, Rabbi **Naftali of Rofshitz**, rose early as usual to make his way to the Rebbe's shul and pour out his heart in prayer to the Creator. On his way home afterwards he passed through the marketplace, where he unexpectedly came upon a peasant farmer with a sack filled with onions!

"Wow!" said Reb Naftoli to himself, struck by a bold idea.

"This is exactly the opportunity I've been waiting for! *Baruch HaShem.*" He approached the gentile and offered to buy the entire sack. The farmer knew very well the value of his precious merchandise and had been looking forward to making a tidy profit. He wasn't going to compromise now. No wholesale discounts! He stated an outrageously high price. To his great surprise, Reb Naftoli instantly agreed and handed him the money.

But that wasn't the end of the surprises. "I'd like to buy your fur coat and hat too," the Rofshitzer added. The farmer couldn't believe his ears. Astonished, he refused. How could he possibly return home in the freezing cold without his coat and hat? But the thick wad of bills in his customer's outstretched hand argued persuasively, and the second deal was also quickly struck. Reb Naftoli strode home with his sack of onions and unusual new items of apparel.

Later that day, a farmer appeared outside the Seer's door. He was clothed in furs, peasant-style, with a huge hat covering his forehead and upper face and boots covered with mud. In the language and intonation of a gentile farmer he called out, "Onions! Onions for sale!"

Chasidim came pouring from every direction. Everyone wanted onions in honor of the holy Shabbat. They crowded around the onion-seller, attempting to bargain with him. He refused to budge from his price. Then, suddenly, he announced that he was stopping for the day. No more onions!

The chasidim pleaded with him. "But we still have to get some for the Rebbe. He is a great, holy man. Blessings will shower upon you, if only you will allow us to buy onions for him."

"If he is as special as you say, I'll do it," rejoined the farmer, "but only if I can sell them to the holy man directly, in person, face-to-face."

The chasidim were shaken. How could they bring such an unrefined character to the Rebbe? After a few moments of confusion, they realized they had no choice. A solemn delegation led the onion-laden farmer to the Seer's house.

When they came in, the Seer was busy polishing his unique *kidush* cup, as he did every Friday before Shabbat. This was an extraordinary chalice, exquisitely crafted of pure gold, with intricate engravings depicting famous sites in the Holy Land, such as the Western Wall, the Tower of David, and the Mount of Olives.

Many rumors surrounded this kidush cup and its history. It was said that the Seer had inherited it from one of the great chasidic masters of the previous generation, and whoever was privileged to make a blessing over its contents and drink from it benefited infinitely. Not that this merit was easy to come by. The Seer did not allow anyone else to use it or even touch it. The whole week it stood in a locked cabinet until Friday, when he would polish it until it glistened and sparkled on the white Shabbat tablecloth.

When his chasidim brought in the gentile with his sack, the Seer understood the reason at once. "How much do you want for your onions?" he queried the farmer.

"One moment. Not so fast," the farmer replied coarsely, holding up his hand as if to ward off the Rebbe's offer. "I'm frozen stiff. I need a proper drink to warm me up."

It was clear that such a person didn't have in mind a cup of tea. The Seer instructed his attendant to serve the man some whisky and a shot glass full to the brim was quickly set down in front of the farmer.

"That's all?" cried out the farmer, as if insulted. Just this little cup?"

"Give him the whole bottle and let him do as he likes," said the Rebbe, turning away.

Now the onion seller seemed mortally offended. "What!

You think I'm a drunkard?" he shouted angrily. "I'll show you! I'll go home. I won't sell you anything!" He tied up the sack and fastened his garments, as if preparing to leave.

The chasidim hurriedly attempted to soothe him, anxiously muttering words of appeasement. Finally he calmed down. Then he smirked. "I'll tell you what," he offered. "I'll sell you my onions if, and only if, you fill this goblet with whisky for me to drink." He pointed at the Rebbe's golden cup shining on the table.

The chasidim drew back, aghast. From this holy *kiddush* cup, which no one dared touch except the Tzadik, this uncircumcised drunken peasant should imbibe his crude booze? They offered him other cups and glasses, bigger ones, singly and in combination, but he was stubborn. "Only from this one, like I told you. Otherwise I go home."

They tried again to dissuade him, but nothing worked. He simply refused to budge. With trembling hands and a heavy heart, the Seer himself filled the precious vessel with the coarse fluid and, with a helpless shrug, presented it to the farmer. The latter lifted it with his right hand, squeezed his eyes shut, and with great concentration and intensity called out, "*Boruch atah ... shehakol neyeh bidvaro.*" *

Everyone was shocked speechless. Only the Seer, after a quick stare, realized what had taken place. A broad smile spread across his face. "*L'chaim*, Reb Naftali! You are so clever. It must be that you deserve to drink from this cup. *L'chaim u'livracha!* — May it be for life and for blessing."

Source: Translated and freely adapted by Yerachmiel Tilles from the Hebrew weekly *Sichat HaShavua*, #74. (First published in *Kfar Chabad Magazine* #847.)]

* The blessing intoned before drinking (except before wine, which has its own blessing).

An All-Purpose Kaddish 20

Biographical notes:

Rabbi **Avraham Benyamin Schreiber**, [of blessed memory: 5575–5635 (1815–1875 C.E.)], known as the ***Ksav Sofer*** — after the title of his halachic responsa, was the son of the illustrious Torah giant, the *Chatam Sofer*, Rabbi Moshe Shreiber, (5522–5599 / 1762–1839 C.E.), and his successor as the head of the Pressburg Yeshiva, the most prestigious in the Austrian-Hungarian empire and the largest in all of Europe.

Rabbi **Yosef Chaim Sonnenfeld** [of blessed memory: 5608– 19 Adar-a 5692 (1848– March 1932 C.E.)], the one from whom we know this story, studied at the Pressburg Yeshiva 1865–1869 C.E. He was a major Torah sage of the Ashkenazi community in the Old City of Jerusalem for nearly sixty years, and its official leader for years after the death of Rabbi Shmuel Salant in 1909.

This story can be related to:

Weekly Readings: *Pinchas* — Numbers 27: 1–4; *Massai* — Numbers 38:10–12 (the orphaning and the betrothals' of the five daughters of Tzlafhad)

Jewish Calendar Date: *Tevet* 10 (the Fast Day on which *Kaddish* is also said for those Holocaust martyrs whose date of death is unknown); The "Three Weeks" (culminating in *Tisha b'Av*—both readings cited above usually fall in this period).

Main Themes: Widows, Kaddish, Conversion

Other Topics: Business, Yeshiva, Orphans, Deeds of kindness, Dreams

An All-Purpose Kaddish

Pressburg was the capital of Hungary for over three centuries, until the formation of the Austro-Hungary Empire in 1867. The yeshiva there, founded by the *Chatam Sofer*, was among the largest and most respected in all of Europe.

In the mid-1800's there lived a wealthy merchant who had a large store in the center of the city. He was well-respected and active in the Jewish community, and also known for his generosity. One charitable custom of his was remarkable. Each day he would count the proceeds of his business, calculate how much was profit, and from that separate 10% as a tithe, which he would deliver daily to the yeshiva.

Tragically, this outstanding man suddenly took ill and passed away at a relatively early age, leaving behind a widow and five young daughters. His wife was a clever and energetic woman who had always helped her husband in the business and knew it well. After his death she took it over and maintained its prosperity. She was also careful to continue in her late husband's generous ways, and each day would deliver the tithe from the profits to the *Rosh Yeshiva* (headmaster), Rabbi **Avraham Benyamin Schreiber**, known as the ***Ksav Sofer***, son of the Chatam Sofer.

Immediately upon her husband's passing, as she had no sons, she asked the Rosh Yeshiva to arrange for Torah scholars to say *kaddish* (a sanctification prayer recited by mourners) for her husband's soul for the entire eleven months, and also each successive year on the *yahrzeit*. She also requested that a second kaddish be said each day, having in mind all those souls who have no one saying kaddish for them.

This went on for nearly ten years. Sometimes the 10% would be as much as hundreds of *kroner* a day, but however much it was, she would always inquire to make sure that the yeshiva was keeping its side of the bargain.

But then the wheel turned. Instead of daily profits there began to be losses. Even so, the widow maintained her schedule of appearing daily at the yeshiva, except that she would inform the Rosh Yeshiva that today, unfortunately, she had nothing to give. Still, she would persist to ask if they were still saying the kaddishes even though she was no longer able to contribute financial support. They would assure her that of course they were, and she should not worry.

Day after day her situation got progressively worse, until finally she had to start selling some of her jewelry and other valuables in order to put food on the table for her daughters. No one was aware of her deteriorating situation except for the senior students and staff of the yeshiva, who knew that her business was virtually bankrupt.

One day a matchmaker came to her house and, after some pleasantries, said, "My dear lady, perhaps because of your extensive involvement in the business you haven't noticed that your daughters have all matured. It is time for them to get married. I am confident that I can find many outstanding yeshiva students that would be interested in them for you to choose from. Just tell me how much dowry you are willing to provide for each one."

She wisely decided not to admit her true situation to him, and instead merely said that she would think it over and then get back to him about his offer. He left, and she burst into tears.

Afterwards, she dressed and hurried to the yeshiva. She poured out her misery to the Rosh Yeshiva. Sobbing, she said, "I just don't understand why my situation deteriorated so." Again, she asked if the kaddishes were still being said, and he comforted her that they were.

Suddenly, the door opened. A distinguished-looking elderly man entered, turned to the widow, and asked her why she was crying. He told her that he knew of her desperate situation and that he was prepared to help. He then requested of the Rosh Yeshiva that they all go into his office and that two scholars of the yeshiva join them. The Rosh Yeshiva acceded, and summoned two of his five great disciples present that year, his son, Rabbi **Shimon Sofer** (subsequently to be known as the *Michtav Sofer*), and Rabbi **Yosef Chaim Sonnenfeld**.**

When they were all assembled, the mysterious guest said, "I know you have five daughters of marriageable age. Let's figure. Each one will need a thousand kroner for dowry money and another thousand kroner each for the expenses of the wedding and for buying furniture and setting up a household. So that is two thousand for each of the five or ten thousand altogether. Plus, to put your business back on its feet, you need another ten thousand kroner, so that makes twenty thousand altogether.

"All right," he said, "I'll write you a check." Whereupon he took a checkbook out of his pocket, tore off a check, wrote the woman's name on it, inscribed it for twenty thousand kroner and signed it! Before handing it to her, however, he asked the two young scholars to sign on the back as witnesses to the transaction. He also asked them to take out their personal notebooks so he could sign in each a sample of his signature, in case the signature on the check would be challenged. Turning back to the woman, he told her that she should present the check at the government bank when it opened at nine o'clock and they would honor it. Then he left, as suddenly as he had come.

All present were shocked, still in disbelief. It was as if they were sharing a dream. Then one of the young rabbis jumped up. "A man like that could really help the yeshiva," he said excitedly, "let's go ask him." The two ran out and searched, but they couldn't find him or anyone who had seen him.

At nine the next morning the widow was at the bank. The

guard at the door directed her to one of the tellers, to whom she showed the check. He looked up the records and told her there were sufficient funds in the account to cover the check, but for such a huge sum he had to first get permission from the manager. He asked her to wait and went to the administrative section. There he presented the check to the head of the bank, who took one look at it and fainted!

Pandemonium broke loose. People were running this way and that. The police came, and after questioning a few employees, confined the astonished woman in a security room and locked the door, pending further investigation.

The doctor that was summoned quickly revived the bank manager. As soon as he gained consciousness, the manager asked that the woman who had brought the check be shown in to him. When told she had been locked up by security, he said that he must go to her. A great mistake had been made to lock up such a righteous woman. He quickly went to her and, after apologizing, invited her to accompany him into his office.

"Tell me, please," he opened, after they were seated, "how did you get this check?"

She told him of her difficulties and the sudden appearance of her unknown benefactor. She explained about her deceased husband and his practice of daily tithing to the yeshiva, and of the kaddishes she had arranged through the yeshiva for him and for those souls who had no one to say kaddish for them.

He asked her if she would see her benefactor again or his picture, would she recognize him? She said yes. She added that two rabbis from the yeshiva were official witnesses to the whole episode and that their signatures were on the back of the check and that the man had also signed their personal notebooks. The manager was excited to hear this, and after looking at their signatures, contacted the yeshiva to ask that Rabbi Sonnenfeld and Rabbi Shimon Sofer come to his office.

They came and confirmed all that the woman had said. The bank manager told the three of them that he would personally honor the check, as it was drawn on his own family account, but that his wife had to endorse it too. He then sent for his wife with the message that she should come quickly because people were waiting for her, but first she should collect all the family photographs in the house and bring them with her.

Although the bank manager was a Jew, his wife was not. When she arrived, he asked the widow and the two rabbis to wait in a different room. He told his wife what was going on and said that they should see if the woman could identify the man who signed the check from among those photographs. She declared that if it all turned out to be true, she would convert to be Jewish.

The manager then spread out all of the photos on his desk. He asked each of the three to enter separately and see if the man who gave the check appeared in any of them. Each one confidently picked out the same person.

The bank manager called everyone in. "Do you know who this man is who gave the check?" he asked. "It is my father, the manager of the bank before me. ...But he has been dead for ten years!

"I must confess," he continued, "that I never said Kaddish for him. Last night he appeared to me in a dream. He said that he had been saved from *Gehinom* (purgatory) by the kaddishes that this woman had arranged for the yeshiva scholars to say for those souls for whom kaddish was not being said, and now that she was in difficulty we had to help her. He said that he would give her a check for twenty thousand kroner, and that if I didn't pay it he would strangle me in my sleep.

"I woke up, frightened. In the morning I told my wife the dream, and she was disturbed too. When the check was shown to me at the bank, I fainted. I knew then that the dream was true.

"I will pay the twenty thousand my father promised. Not only that," he added, turning to the woman, "I will add another twenty thousand of my own, because you fulfilled my obligation for me, and helped my deceased father's soul with the kaddish-saying you arranged."

He addressed the three of them again. "I fully regret my lapse from Judaism. I see now that our G-d is the one, true G-d, and He gives to all their just reward. I resolve that from now on I will fulfill His commandments as revealed in our Torah. My wife, too, has reaffirmed her promise to convert, and to live in accordance with Jewish law." Turning to the two rabbis, he added, "I hope you will guide us to understand what we have to do."

He instructed the teller to give the woman forty thousand kroner. The first thing she did was to give ten percent of it to the yeshiva. Soon thereafter, her business waxed prosperous again, and her five daughters married G-d-fearing young Torah scholars.

Source: Translated and freely adapted by Yerachmiel Tilles from *Otzar Hamasiyot* by Reuven Nena, vol. I, pp. 42–47, in the name of Rabbi Y. Shapira of Jerusalem, who heard it from Rabbi Sonnenfeld himself. (First published on *AscentOf Safed. com*, in 5758/ 1997.)

Translator's note:

—

* Another teller of the story writes that the witness besides Rabbi Sonnenfeldwas Rabbi Yehoshua Greenwald, who became Chief Rabbi of Austro-Hungary, and not Rabbi Shimon Sofer.

21 The Most Desirable Apples

Biographical notes for this story:

Rabbi **Chaim Halberstam of Sanz** [of blessed memory: 25 Nissan 5553– 25 Nissan 5636 (April 1793– April 1876 C.E.)] was the first Rebbe of the Sanz-Klausenberg dynasty. He is a renowned Torah scholar and famous for his extraordinary dedication to the mitzvah of tzedaka. His voluminous and wide-ranging writings were all published under the title *Divrei Chaim*. His eldest son, the *Divrei Yehezkel* of Shinova, founded the famous Sanzer synagogue in Tzefat in the middle 1800's.

This story can be related to:

Weekly Readings: *Bahar* — Leviticus. 25:35 ("If your brother becomes impoverished and cannot support himself, you must come to his aid").

Jewish Calendar Date: *Nissan* 25 (a few days after *Pesach* ends) — birth and *yahrzeit* of the Divrei Chaim

Main Themes: Deeds of kindness

Other Topics: Buying and selling, Marketplace, Apples, Humility

19th Century (2nd half) Eastern Europe

The Most Desirable Apples

ONE DAY LATE in the week, a poor woman who was from a well-respected Jewish family knocked on the door of the ***Divrei Chaim* of Sanz**. She requested his financial help, saying plaintively that she had yet to accrue sufficient funds to purchase the necessities for Shabbat.

The Divrei Chaim was surprised. "Don't you have a stall for selling apples in the marketplace?" he asked. "Why is it that you have no money?"

She explained that people were saying that her apples were of inferior quality, and as a result she had hardly been able to sell any this week.

When the Rebbe heard the cause of her problem, he rose and, adorned in his elegant rabbinic robe and chasidic hat, strode off to the woman's stall in the marketplace. The shoppers were astonished to see him there and word of it spread quickly.

The Rebbe ignored their stares and calmly assumed a place behind the seller's table. "My fellow Jews!" he called out. "Here are good apples for sale ... very good apples ... excellent apples. Who wants to buy them?"

Immediately there was a jostling stampede towards the apple-vendor's table. People offered two, three, ten times the official price of the apples, because everybody wanted to buy the fruit directly from the hand of the holy Divrei Chaim of Sanz. In a very short time all the apples were sold for exorbitant amounts, and the Rebbe handed over to the woman a sum of money so large she could barely believe that it had come only from her apples.

"Look," said the Rebbe, "your apples were of good quality. It is just that the townspeople didn't realize it until today."

Source: Translated-supplemented by Yerachmiel Tilles from *Sipurei Chasidim-Torah* (#299) by Rabbi S. Y. Zevin. (First published on *AscentOf Safed. com.*)

The Farmer Method

Biographical notes for this story:

Rabbi **Shmuel Schneersohn** [of blessed memory: 2 Iyar 5594– 13 Tishrei 5643 (1834– Sept. 1882 C.E.)], the fourth Lubavitch Rebbe, known as the ***Rebbe Maharash***, was the seventh and youngest son of his predecessor, Rabbi Menachem Mendel Schneersohn, the *Tsemach Tsedek*.

Rabbanit **Menucha-Rachel Slonim**, for many decades the matriarch of the Ashkenazi Jewish community in Hevron, was the daughter of the second Lubavitcher Rebbe, Rabbi Dov Ber Schneuri. She and her husband, Rabbi Yaakov Slonim, were sent to Hevron by the Rebbe in the early 1800's to bolster its fledging Chabad congregation (originally started by fifteen Chabad families who moved there from Tzefat).

This story can be related to:

Weekly Readings: *Ekev* — Deuteronomy 11:12 ("A land which G-d cares for, ... keeps a constant eye upon it...")

The Jewish Holidays: *Cheshvan* 7 (2 weeks after Shemini Atzeret) — the day the prayers for rain begin in Israel

Jewish Calendar Date: *Iyar* 2 (10 days after *Pesach; Teiferet sh'b'tiferet* in the *Omer* count) — birth date of Rebbe Maharash; *Tishrei* 13 (2 days before Sukkot) — his *yahrzeit.*

Main Themes: Israel, Rain

Other Topics: Jerusalem, Prayer, Farming, Innocence

The Farmer Method

A CHABAD CHASID from the Slonim family in the Holy Land once sailed to White Russia to visit the Lubavitcher Rebbe of that time, the *Maharash*, who was also his relative. The Rebbe asked him many questions about the situation of the Jews in the Land. While answering, the chasid commented, "I don't understand what is written in certain books that in the Holy Land dwell lofty souls. I knew the Jews there, and I haven't seen that they are more special than the Jews here."

"Oh, are you qualified to recognize lofty souls?" remarked the Rebbe. "Here, let me tell you a story that I heard from my father, the Rebbe [the *Tzemech Tzedek*] of blessed memory, about a simple Jew in the Land of Israel.

There was once a Jewish farmer who lived just outside of Jerusalem. He did not know how to study Torah, nor did he even understand the words of the prayers that he said everyday. In fact, he couldn't grasp the order of the prayers. To tell him that there was a different Psalm each day and longer *Tachanun* penitential prayers on Mondays and Thursdays than on the other weekdays, except on those days when they are not said at all, left him hopelessly confused. Instead, when he came to the city once a week to sell his produce, he would go to one of the local rabbis, who would write down for him the order of the prayers for each of the seven days to come.

One year, in the month of Mar-Cheshvan, when the rainy season usually begins, he asked the rabbi to list for him two weeks' worth. He explained that because of the bad road conditions caused by the winter rains, he would now come only once every two weeks.

It turned out, however, that he came to Jerusalem the next week anyway. He had something pressing to attend to, and besides, it hadn't rained. When he arrived, he halted his donkey in shock. All the Jewish stores were closed!

The simple fellow was seized by anxiety. Could he possibly have miscounted the days? G-d have mercy! Was it Shabbat today? He stood motionless. What could he do?

Looking around, he saw a solitary Jew on the street, walking along with his *tallit* and *tefillin* under his arm. "Thank G-d!" the farmer intoned; "It can't be Shabbat if he is carrying tefillin!"

But if so, why were the stores closed and the street deserted? He approached the strolling Jew he had spotted and asked him what was going on. The man told him that it was a public fast day.

Now he felt distressed again. A fast day? But he had already eaten! And failed to say the appropriate extra prayers too. Why hadn't the rabbi warned him the week before?

Abandoning his donkey and wagon right in the middle of the marketplace where he had stopped, he rushed over to the rabbi's house. There he was told that the rabbi was still in shul, so off he ran again, his heart pounding from both fear and exertion. "Rabbi!" he cried out, bursting into tears. "How could you do this to me!"

The rabbi couldn't understand why he was so upset. "What happened, my friend?" he asked gently.

"'What happened?' you ask? Today is a fast day, I just found out, but Your Honor didn't write it down or even mention anything about it to me last week, and so I already ate and said the wrong prayers. Woe is me!"

The rabbi smiled, relieved. "You can relax, my friend. This is not a regular fast day. We just recently decreed this special fast day for the residents of Jerusalem because of the possibility of a serious drought due to our lack of rain, but you don't live here and so were in no way obligated."

The farmer looked perplexed. "When you folks need rain, you decree a *fast*?" he asked, puzzled.

"That's right," the rabbi replied.

"Really?"

"Of course. Why is that surprising? What do *you* think we should do?"

"Well," answered the farmer, innocently, "when my fields don't have enough rain, I go out there and say to the One Above, 'Father! I need rain, and then it starts to rain."

The Rabbi looked at the simple looking fellow intensely and saw that he was sincere. "If that's so, why don't you try and see if your methods will work here in the city too."

The farmer turned and went outside to the courtyard of the shul. He began to weep. Through his tears he cried out, "Father! Can it possibly be that the people of your Holy City will expire from famine? Don't You see that they need rain?"

Immediately the sky darkened and rain began to fall.

As he completed the story, the *Maharash* said to his visitor from the Holy Land, "So do you really think you are able to distinguish who in the Land is a lofty soul?"

Source: Translated and freely adapted by Yerachmiel Tilles from *Sippurei Chasidim-Torah* #302 by Rabbi S. Y. Zevin. (First published on *AscentOf Safed.com*.)

A Surgical Procedure 23

Biographical note for this story:

Rabbi **Yehoshua Rokeach of Belz,** [of blessed memory: 5585– 23 Shvat 5654 (1825– January 1894 C.E.)] was the fifth son and the successor to his father, Rabbi Sholom, the first Rebbe of Belz. A major leader of Galician Jewry, he was also the founder of *Machzikei HaDas,* perhaps the first Orthodox Jewish organization to be involved in government politics that is still a force in Israel today. Some of his discourses have been published in *Ohel Yehoshua*, a supplement to the book of his father's teachings, *Dover Sholom*. He was succeeded by his second son, Yissachar Dov, grandfather of today's Belzer Rebbe, who bears his name.

This story can be related to:

Weekly Readings: *Mishpatim* — Exodus 21:19 ("...he shall provide for his cure" — Onkelos translation: "He shall pay the doctor's fee.")

Jewish Calendar Date: *Shvat* 23 (8 days after *Tu b'Shvat*) — *yahrzeit* of Rebbe Yehoshua of Belz

Main Themes: Surgery, Moshiach

Other Topics: Illness, University, Becoming a chasid

A Surgical Procedure

In 1854 C.E., Rabbi **Yehoshua Rokeach,** The Belzer Rebbe, suffered from a succession of mysterious ailments. Although he was in much pain, he maintained a cheerful countenance. His chasidim, however, were greatly worried, not just because of the illnesses themselves, for they were all curable, but because of certain disturbing hints from the Rebbe that his end was near.

The next time the Rebbe's condition worsened, they decided to spare no expense and bring him to Vienna. There, they took him to the finest medical facility in Europe, to be examined by top specialists. The doctors announced their diagnosis: an immediate and risky operation was urgently necessary.

The Belzer Rebbe made his preparations. He immersed in the *mikveh*, he wrote his will, and he recited with great emotion the words of the Final Confession. Only then, in an exalted spirit, did he allow himself to be placed on the operating table.

The surgical team assembled around the Rebbe. All awaited the chief surgeon's signal to the anesthetist to begin his procedure.

Suddenly, to everyone's surprise, the Rebbe called out to one of the surgeons. And, after confirming his first name, he said: "Moses? You're a Jew, aren't you?" The doctor quietly nodded his head.

Moses, whose given name was actually *Moshe Yitzchak*, was from a small town called Linden. There he had grown up in a traditional Jewish home. His father had tried his best to provide him with a strong Jewish education, but alas, the boy's heart was drawn in a completely different direction. As his head filled with visions of more cosmopolitan, attracting vistas, he grew further and further from the values of his nurturing home. As soon as he was of age, he left Linden and his distraught parents, and headed for the great metropolis of Vienna.

The first step he took in his new life was to change his name to Moses. Next, he enrolled in a secular school, where thanks to his brilliant mind and determined diligence, he caught up to and surpassed others his age by absorbing an extraordinarily large amount of material in a relatively short period of time.

Armed with his degree, he was accepted to the medical school of the university, and there too he was highly successful. Soon after, he became established as a first-class physician and surgeon.

Unfortunately, the more he succeeded, the further he drifted from his Jewish roots. No longer could anyone recognize that the sophisticated Dr. Moses was the small-town Moshe Yitzchak of Linden.

Although Moses' nod of affirmation of his Jewish identity was small and unobtrusive, it was noticed by everyone in the room. There was absolute silence when the Rebbe continued, "Moses, do you believe that G-d Al-mighty created the world and conducts it?" After a short hesitation the perplexed Moses answered, "Yes, Rabbi, I do."

The medical staff looked on in astonishment, but the Rebbe seemed oblivious to their stares as all his attention was focused on the doctor. "And what about *Moshiach,* the righteous one, who will come at any moment and redeem our people from the exile? Do you believe that, Moses?"

This time Moses was silent longer. He selected his words carefully. "Uh, I believe that there will come a certain time when there will be a redemption, but I don't believe that it will come about through a Messiah, a single person, who will rule over the whole world and everyone will be in awe and fear of him. Such a thing is not within the realm of rational possibility, so I can't accept it."

The Belzer lifted his head and turned to face Moses directly. He opened wide his powerful eyes, two bright shining orbs radiating kindness and goodness, but also power and authority.

The Rebbe's penetrating gaze fastened on Moses. He felt it burning into him. He tried to avert his own eyes but was unable. It was as if they were magnetically attached to those of the Rebbe.

The stunned members of the medical team saw their comrade's face turn deathly pale, then blush bright as a beet. Then white again, and then red again. His whole body was trembling and his hands began to shake. They had no idea what to think of this unexpected bizarre interaction, but they realized Moses must be undergoing some sort of spiritual or emotional trauma.

The tension was palpable. Moses was panting and breathing with difficulty as if he had just completed a long-distance run. He tried his best to calm himself and relax, but found himself unable to. The simple fact that someone had asserted control over him with just a glance kept him in internal turmoil.

Finally, the Rebbe averted his eyes from Moses. The surgeon felt his composure return. Then the Rebbe looked at him again, and studied his face, but this time his gaze was caressing. "*Nu*, Moses, now do you believe that an individual is capable of arousing fear in all those around him with just a glance of the eyes?"

Moses nodded in silent admission.

"Well, Moses, that is exactly how it will be when *Moshiach* arrives. G-d's chosen one will rule over the entire world, and everyone will abandon his evil ways and turn towards G-d."

"The Rebbe is right. I was mistaken," muttered the shaken physician.

The drama over, the operation was ready to take place. Afterwards, it was pronounced a great success, and thousands of chasidim breathed sighs of relief.

Fifteen days later, the Belzer Rebbe was discharged. He boarded the train to return to Belz from Vienna. To the deep sorrow of his followers, however, he never arrived, but went to his eternal reward during the course of the journey on 23 Shvat, at age 59. Among those that merited to be in the small group of disciples present at the moment that the Rebbe passed on was his devoted chasid, Moshe Yitzchak of Linden.

Source: Translated and freely adapted by Yerachmiel Tilles from the Hebrew weekly *Sichat HaShavua*, #556. (First published in *Kfar Chabad Magazine* #784.)

Silence Speaks 24

Biographical notes for this story:

Rabbi **Yisroel** (ben Baruch) **Hager of Vizhnitz**, Bokovina [of blessed memory: 5620– 2 Sivan 5696 (1860– May 1936 C.E.)], had many thousands of followers over the 43 years he served as Rebbe. After WWI he headed a major yeshiva in Hungary. Because of his warmth and friendliness to every Jew, he was known as "the *Ahavas Yisroel*".

This story can be related to:

Weekly Readings: *Kedoshim* — Leviticus 19:17 ("...Rebuke you shall rebuke your fellow..."); *Mishpatim* — Exodus 22:21 ("Do not mistreat a widow or an orphan.")

Jewish Calendar Date: *Sivan* 2 (4 days before *Shavuot*) — *yahrzeit* of Rebbe Yisrael of Vizhnitz

Main Themes: Rebuke, Deeds of kindness

Other Topics: Exercise, Widows

24

20th Century
(1st half)
Eastern Europe

Silence Speaks

It happened about a hundred years ago. Every weekday evening Rabbi **Yisroel Hager**, the saintly *Vizhnitzer Rebbe*, would go out for a stroll for about half an hour, accompanied by one of his attendants. One day, much to the surprise of his *shammash* (attendant), the Rebbe stopped in front of a large house next to the town park belonging to the manager of the local bank, went up the steps, and knocked on the door.

The attendant had no idea what the Rebbe could possibly want in the house of the bank manager. The banker was most certainly not a chasid. In fact, he was one of the local leaders of the *Haskalah* (Reformed Enlightenment movement opposed to traditional Judaism). Nevertheless, when he saw the door open and the butler usher the Rebbe in, he quickly raced up the steps and slipped into the house too, not willing for the Rebbe to be left alone and unattended.

The bank manager came downstairs and couldn't believe his eyes, the Vizhnitzer Rebbe in his house! He greeted his guest warmly, showed him to a comfortable chair in the salon, and sat down opposite him. After some initial pleasantries, he waited for the Rebbe to state the reason for his unexpected call.

A few minutes passed in silene. The host became a bit uncomfortable. A refined cosmopolitan man, he would never presume to confront his distinguished guest about why he had come. Excusing himself, he walked to a position where the Rebbe couldn't see him, and frantically signalled to the Rebbe's attendant to join him in the hall.

"Why on earth did the Rabbi come here?"

"I have no idea. The Rebbe didn't tell me anything. I saw him enter, so I followed him in."

Perplexed, the bank manager returned to his seat. He looked at the Rebbe. The Rebbe looked at him. More silence. What was going on?

The host was finding it increasingly difficult to maintain his sophisticated constraint. Finally, after several more minutes, the Rebbe stood up. Still not saying a word, he walked towards the door. Displaying good manners, the bank manager escorted him out. He followed the Rebbe down the steps and several paces along the sidewalk, started to turn back but almost instantly reconsidered, and continued to follow behind the calmly strolling tzadik.

When they reached the Rebbe's house and the Rebbe paused to start up the steps, the bank manager finally threw off all restraint and called out, "Vizhnitzer Rebbe! Please excuse me for asking, but why did you come to my house? While you were my guest I would never presume to pry, but now we are at *your* house, so I can ask you."

The Rebbe turned slowly towards him. "I came to your house to fulfill a *mitzvah*. Thank G-d, I succeeded."

"Which mitzvah?"

"Our sages say that just as it is a mitzvah to speak out when you will be listened to,* so it is a mitzvah to not say anything when you know you will not be listened to.

"But what does it mean to not say anything?" the Rebbe continued. "To sit in your house in silence? Not at all. You have to go to the person to whom you are not supposed to say what he won't listen to, confront him face-to-face, and then refrain from saying it!

"And that," concluded the Rebbe, "is precisely what I did."

"So what is it that you did not say?" queried the bewildered bank manager.

The attendant, standing by respectfully, was equally curious to know.

"I can't tell you that," the tzadik insisted.

"Why not?"

"Because then I will lose my mitzvah!"

"But how do you know that I wouldn't listen?"

"I know."

"But you can't know that. You *must* tell me what it is!" pleaded the bank manager, totally overcome by curiosity.

"I'm sorry. No," said the Rebbe firmly

After several more rounds, the bank manager begged: "Please, please, please, at least give me a chance."

"Oh, all right," said the Rebbe with a show of reluctance. "Yesterday, a distraught woman, recently widowed, came to speak to me. Apparently, she received a notice signed by you that your bank has decided to put her house up for auction next week because she is unable to pay the mortgage. That means she and her little children will be out on the street. She asked me to speak to you, because she knows that you are Jewish. She hoped I could influence you to have compassion on her and her children.

"I, however, did not bring it up to you because of the mitzvah to not say."

"But Rebbe," exclaimed the banker in frustration, "You don't understand! It's not *me* she owes, it's the bank. I don't *own* the bank, I only manage it; I don't set policy. Besides—"

"Right," the Rebbe interrupted. "As I said. I knew you wouldn't listen. Good night."

The Rebbe walked up the steps to his dwelling, followed by his attendant. The door closed behind them. The bank manager stood immobile, stunned. Finally, he walked home, alone and bemused, but the matter had entered his heart and he was unable to dismiss it.

Before the week was up, he paid the widow's entire mortgage out of his own personal account.

Source: Translated and freely adapted by Yerachmiel Tilles from *Sipurei Chasidim-Torah* (# 147) by Rabbi S. Y. Zevin. (First published on *AscentOfSafed.com*.)

Translator's note:

—

* Look up *Leviticus* 19:17 and its commentaries.

25 "Him — Not Him"

Biographical note for this story:

Rabbi **Sholom-Dovber Schneersohn** [of blessed memory: 20 Cheshvan 5621– 2 Nissan 5610 (Oct. 1860– April 1920 C.E.)], known as the ***Rebbe Reshab***, was the fifth Rebbe of the Lubavitcher dynasty. He is the author of hundreds of major tracts in the exposition of chasidic thought.

This story can be related to:

Weekly Readings: *Netzavim* — Deuteronomy 30:3–4 ("He will bring back your remnants from among all the nations ... even at the ends of Heaven....")

Jewish Calendar Date: *Nissan* 2 (two weeks before Pesach) — *yahrzeit* of the Rebbe Reshab

Main Themes: Mathematics, University

Other Topics: Torah study, Zohar, Non-Jews, Anti-semitism, Police, Becoming a chasid

"Him — Not Him"

About a hundred years ago in a village in Russia, there lived a student named Yaakov who was exceptionally bright, and who dedicated himself to Torah study with considerable success.

In the same village lived a number of Lubavitcher chasidim, who often tried to persuade Yaakov to accompany them to their rebbe. Yaakov, who was not from a chasidic home, always refused. "What do I need a rebbe for?" he would say. "Even when I have a difficulty understanding some complexity in Gamorra, I just work on it a little harder and I am able to get the answer by myself."

Nevertheless, one time Yaakov yielded to the urging of the chasidim, and agreed to accompany them to Lubavitch, to the **Rebbe Reshab**. Arriving there on Friday, they passed the Shabbat in an exalted atmosphere that was unfamiliar but attractive to Yaakov.

Saturday night, the travelling chasidim lined up to part from the Rebbe. Yaakov, according to the custom explained to him, also wrote a *kvittel,* (a personal note), to present to the Rebbe during his private audience. As his turn approached, he surprised himself by how excited with anticipation he was.

Yaakov entered and saw the Rebbe sitting at his desk, concentrating on a book. The Rebbe didn't even glance at him. Yaakov, unsure of what to do, tiptoed up to the desk and placed his note on it. The Rebbe's eyes never left his book, as if he didn't notice a thing.

Suddenly the Rebbe stood up and started pacing back and forth. To Yaakov's surprise he heard the Rebbe muttering, as if he were talking to himself, but in Russian. "*Ohn*!" ("It is him"). "*Nyeh ohn*!" ("It's not him"). "It is him. It's not him. It..." The Rebbe was silent for a moment, and then pronounced in a firm, decisive voice, "*Nyeh ohn* — it's not him." Then the Rebbe sat back down and resumed reading his book, still not acknowledging Yaakov's presence.

Yaakov backed out of the room, totally confused. Not only had the Rebbe completely ignored him, but what was the significance of the Russian litany the Rebbe had muttered? It was a strange riddle, and he had no clue as to its meaning.

Time passed. One day Yaakov noticed in a newspaper an intricate mathematical problem, presented by the university in Petersberg. They were offering a three hundred ruble prize for whoever could solve it. The young talmudic scholar took it as a personal challenge and devoted a serious effort to solving it. Finally he got it! He mailed in his answer to the university.

Shortly thereafter he received a notification that his solution was correct and that he would be awarded the stipulated prize. The envelope also contained an invitation to meet with the chairman of the Mathematics Department in Petersberg, together with a train ticket for the journey.

Yaakov went. The department chairman and the other representatives of the university were astonished to see that the mathematical wizard of their correspondence was a young religious Jew, wearing traditional garb. However, they were quickly captivated by his incisive intelligence. After they presented him the three hundred ruble prize, they invited him to remain at the university and complete a degree in mathematics, under a full scholarship.

Impressed by the generosity of the proposal, Yaakov accepted. He enrolled as a student at the university in Petersberg, and launched into the studies.

At first Yaakov was steadfast in maintaining his Jewish appearance and ways. He even managed to maintain a daily session of Torah. As he progressed in his secular studies, however, and as his academic and social status grew, he gradually fell away from his Torah lifestyle. He spent his free time with his colleagues, who taught him new pastimes.

The first to go were the external signs: his distinctive clothing, his beard and so forth. Next he gave up learning Torah. Eventually, he ceased observing *mitzvot* too.

After several more years, Yaakov was offered a full professorship in the mathematics department. There was only one hitch. In order to gain the position he would have to convert. Well, he wasn't going to let that one little detail hold him back from such a prestigious appointment.

As time went by, Yaakov's conscience began to plague him. How could he have done such a deed? He heartily regretted it. Nevertheless, he found himself unable to commit himself to rectify the situation. Not only were there the obvious social and economic penalties, but in that era in Russia if a Jew who converted to Christianity were to convert back (or if a gentile converted to Judaism) it was considered a capital crime, subject to immediate execution.

Lately Yaakov found himself going hunting more and more often. He enjoyed this 'sport' he had learned from his gentile friends in Petersberg. Now it served to relax him, and provide brief respite from the anguish of his soul. One day, while he was in the saddle, his horse suddenly started to gallop wildly. Yaakov lost all control as the horse galloped even faster and more recklessly. He felt that unless a miracle happened this would be his end. At that moment, he made a firm promise to himself that if he were to be saved, he would return to being Jewish and do complete *tshuvah*.

Amazingly, as soon as he made this resolution, the horse calmed down and slowed to a canter.

That very night, Yaakov gathered some money and a bundle of his possessions, walked out on his non-Jewish wife, and departed for parts unknown. He wandered incognito from town to town and from village to village, nervously reacting to every falling leaf. He knew that with his return to Judaism he had endangered his life, but he had made his decision and he had no intention of going back.

One day, when he was eating a meal in an out-of-the-way inn, several policemen suddenly burst in and began checking everyone's personal documents. Since Yaakov had no identity papers, he was arrested and taken for interrogation.

Opposite him in the small room a cruel-faced investigator sat at his table. He stared at Yaakov, looked down at the picture in his hand, and then at Yaakov's face again. Out of the corner of his eye, Yaakov recognized that it was a photograph of him as he looked when he was a professor at the university, clean-shaven, with a modern hairdo and nattily dressed. He looked quite different now, but still....

The investigator hesitated. Yaakov felt his fate closing upon him.

Suddenly, the investigator began a dialogue with himself. "*Ohn*! *Nyeh ohn*! It is him. It's not him. It is him. It's not him. It is him." Yaakov remembered well where he had first heard those words, when, and from whom. They rang in his head like a bell. He held his breath. Back and forth the investigator repeated: "It is him. It's not him. It is him." Finally he decided: "*Nyeh ohn*!" — "It's not him," and ordered the Jew's release.

Yaakov could barely believe it. He was saved! Within a short time he set off for Lubavitch, and once there, he never departed.

Source: Translated-retold by Yerachmiel Tilles from the Hebrew weekly *Sichat HaShavua* #567, based on *Rabboseinu Nasienu* by R. Yosef Yitzchak Kamenetzky. (First published in *Kfar Chabad Magazine* #783.)

PART IV

20th Century (C.E.): Chasidic Masters and Other Jewish Heroes

A Soul's Scream 26

This story can be related to:

Weekly Readings: *Vaet'chanan* — Deuteronomy 6:4 ("*Shma, Yisrael* … G-D is one")

Jewish Calendar Date: *Tevet* 10 (the Fast Day on which *Kaddish* is also said for those Holocaust martyrs whose date of death is unknown)

Main Themes: Holocaust

Other Topics: *Shma Yisrael*

A Soul's Scream

I WAS IN A CONCENTRATION CAMP in Hungary, near the Romanian border, under the rule of the accursed Nazis. When their defeat was all but official, and the once-mighty German war machine was retreating in the face of the advancing Russian troops, rumors increased of the imminent arrival of the Russians. I and two others decided to attempt to escape from the sinister clasp of the Nazis, and hopefully reach the nearby and presumably friendlier arms of the Russians before the Germans could catch us.

Eliezer HaKohein Isaac told this amazing account of his World War II experience to his son-in-law, Yitzchak Hershkovitz, of Petach Tikvah.

Our plan was to sneak over at twilight, one by one, to the corral at the edge of the camp where the horses were kept. Then, as soon as it became dark, we would run as fast as we could into the nearby forest. The plot was fraught with danger, and we well understood that if apprehended we would immediately be hanged, but the temptation of possible success outweighed our fear. We prepared ourselves in eager anticipation and waited, day after day, for the right moment to execute our plan.

One evening, the guards seemed lax in their attention. We decided that this was our chance! Carefully, we slipped over to the corral at intervals. Each of us carried a brush for grooming the horses. If anyone stopped us, we would say we had come to care for the animals.

As soon as it became dark, we sprinted toward the forest. Much to our relief, no alarm was raised. No one had even noticed! Nevertheless, we knew we didn't have much time until our disappearance would become known and the pursuit would begin. So when we reached the forest, we decided to keep running for as long as our strength held out in the direction we desperately estimated that the Russians were coming.

For several hours we trotted through the thick forest. Suddenly we heard frightening sounds from behind us, in the distance. Quickly, we climbed three tall trees nearby, as high as we could, and waited nervously for what fate would bring.

The sounds became louder as their source drew closer. It was the barking of dogs! After a while, we saw German soldiers pounding down the route we had taken, with ferocious dogs on leashes. Thank heaven, neither soldiers nor animals noticed us as they whipped past our trees and continued deeper into the forest.

The leaves on the branches of our lofty perches were fluttering in the chilly night wind, and we too were shaking, but with fear. Nevertheless, we dared to hope that the Nazi beasts would not expend much more time hunting for us. The chances of finding us in the pitch darkness of the forest were too slim, and they would have to worry about running into the advancing Soviet troops. And so it was. After an hour or two, we saw them heading back in the direction of the camp.

Even after they were gone, we remained in our trees for a while, until we were absolutely convinced that none of our pursuers had remained in the area. Only then did we carefully descend to the ground, and resume trekking into the heart of the forest. Although we were already weak and exhausted, we pushed ourselves to keep moving until daylight penetrated the dense green overhead. Then, after some looking about, we found a well-hidden pit where, on the verge of imminent collapse, we felt confident enough to curl up and sleep.

At dusk, we emerged from our place of concealment and began to walk again. For three days we traveled by night and slept during the day, sustaining ourselves with berries that grew wild in the forest.

Towards morning of the fourth day, we spotted in the distance a clearing in the forest, with a house rooted firmly in the middle of it. We approached it as silently and inconspicuously as we could, and spied it from all sides. We didn't detect any signs of life whatsoever. Convincing each other that it was safe, we gathered our nerve and entered.

After exploring every room, we concluded that the house was indeed abandoned. We went up to the roof and spread out thin mattresses of straw. After three days in the forest, we were overjoyed to be able to pamper our weary bones and rest properly. Exhausted and physically broken, within a few minutes all three of us were sound asleep in a deep slumber.

I don't know how many hours we slept, but our wakening was instantaneous and frightening. The door crashed loudly open with a kick! If it was Germans, we were doomed. Even if they were Russian soldiers, it might not help us much. They tended to shoot first and ask questions later.

As we bolted upright, I heard a scream of "*Sh'ma Yisrael*," followed immediately by a quick order barked in Russian. Three Russian officers appeared in our line of vision, led by an officer. The muzzles of their rifles were aimed directly at our foreheads.

We froze. It took me a few seconds to sort out my perceptions, whereupon I realized that the piercing shout of "Sh'ma Yisrael" had come from Bernhard, while the order in Russian had burst forth from the officer.

It turned out that they were a patrol whose job was to hunt for German soldiers trying to escape or in hiding. The commanding officer was actually a Jewish doctor, who was serving in the Russian army. As soon as he heard "*Sh'ma Yisrael*," he had instinctively roared the command, "Hold your fire."

Amazing! Bernhard's cry from the depths of his soul had saved our three lives. The most surprising thing was that he, unlike myself and our other companion, was a totally non-religious assimilated Jew! In fact, only his mother was Jewish, which had made him just half-Jewish in the eyes of our cruel captors, and as such wore a white ribbon on his arm instead of a yellow one.

To this day, two questions from this harrowing turning point in my life gnaw at my mind. Why didn't the quick-triggered Russians shoot us as soon as they spotted us on the roof? And how could it be that Bernhard, an assimilated Jew in his own eyes as well as in everyone else's, was the one who cried out *Sh'ma* so quickly and instinctively?

I guess I'll never know, but one thing I certainly learned from that incredible episode. Hidden in the heart of every Jew, no matter how assimilated, is an extraordinary Jewish soul, waiting to assert itself at the moment of truth.

Source: Translated-adapted by Yerachmiel Tilles from the Hebrew weekly *Sichat Hashavua*, #604. (First published in *Kfar Chabad Magazine* #838.)

Only Mine 27

This story can be related to:

Weekly Readings: *Vayera* — Genesis ch. 22 (the "*Akeida*" — "the binding of Isaac")

The Jewish Holidays: *Rosh Hashana* (2nd day, we read the *Akeidas Yitzchak* section)

Jewish Calendar Date: *Tevet* 10 (the Fast Day on which *Kaddish* is also said for those Holocaust martyrs whose date of death is unknown)

Main Themes: Holocaust

Other Topics: Children, *Akeida* (see above)

Only Mine

It was in the waning days of the Warsaw Ghetto. The Elbaum family, Yisrael, Chaya, and their only child, Tamar, had secreted themselves in a bunker. There they were relatively secure, but now the problem arose that they had depleted their small stash of food. Someone would have to emerge, go to the streets, and try to acquire some food in order for the family to survive.

The only logical choice was little Tamareleh. A young child was much less likely to be noticed by the Nazi beasts than an adult. Early in the morning, before dawn, Tamareleh crept out, to begin her search for food for herself and her parents.

Alas, her parents had no way of knowing that this same morning the German invaders would conduct one of their notorious roundups. They broke into houses and arrested every Jew they spotted on the streets, herding them all into Umschlagplatz. A shudder went through the Ghetto. From Umschlagplatz there was only one known destination, the hellhole named Treblinka.

The Nazis had already captured and assembled a large number of men, women, and children. The cries of the children separated from their parents broke the hearts of all the adults. Nevertheless, they held back the little ones who tried to run home, for fear that the vicious Nazis would shoot them on the spot.

Word of the raid reached the Elbaums. They became paralyzed with worry for Tamareleh, for hours had gone by and she had not yet returned. They couldn't but think that,G-d forbid, she too had been captured. They stared at the entrance to the bunker, reacting nervously to every small sound from that direction.

As the minutes and hours ticked away, Yisrael and Chaya felt as if the sky was about to fall on their heads. The only light in the oppressive darkness of their tragic lives was their precious Tamareleh. Their strong love for her was all that kept them going, and now they had to face the inescapable conclusion that she too was among the forlorn souls isolated under the German guns in Umshlagplatz. They realized they had to try everything in their power to save her.

With fierce determination they slid out from their hiding place. They understood they had no viable way to save their daughter from the vicious Nazi beasts, but it was not logic that was determining their choices. Their parental drive could not be suppressed, but what could they do?

Then Yisrael had an idea. He remembered that an acquaintance of his, named Perlstein, was a member of the Jewish police of the Ghetto. He even knew his daughter, and at times had showed her affection. Maybe this *kapo* could be her rescuer, they hoped. They were so excited they wished they could tunnel through the walls of all the intervening structures to reach Perlstein's dwelling! In that building, 9 Dejilna Street, lived most of the Jewish policemen and their families.

When Perlstein answered the frantic knocking on the door, he was surprised to see the Elbaum couple standing there. They quickly poured out the tragic story of Tamar's capture, and he took it very much to heart. For a few minutes a heavy silence dominated the room where they spoke. They could see that the policeman was racking his brain to try to come up with a plan to rescue little Tamareleh.

Suddenly, Perlstein's features became very animated. He swept his police uniform cap off of his head, pulled his police identification card out of his pocket, and thrust the two of them into the hand of an astonished Yisrael Elbaum.

"Take these and run to Umshlagplatz. Run!" he emphasized, "Before it is too late. Tell the policemen there that your daughter is among the captured, and they will help you to get her released and take her away. This is an unwritten law among us: no snatching the children of the policemen."

Perlstein understood very well that by this maneuver he was endangering his own life. But the beseeching faces of the frantic couple compelled him to offer this slim chance, despite the personal risk to himself.

Yisrael stared at Perlstein as if he were a dream apparition. It seemed such a simple, yet foolproof plan.

His heart began to beat with hope. His wife began to cry in happy expectation and his eyes, too, filled with tears. Could it really be that in a short time they would have their precious Tamareleh back? They tried to express their gratitude to Perlstein but the words wouldn't come. Anyway, he cut them off quickly, insisting there was no more time to talk. They must hurry.

Yisrael put on the police cap, and stuck the document in his pocket. He was halfway out the door when Perlstein called his name. He turned his head and the kapo said to him, "One moment. There is one thing that I forgot to tell you. It is already so late. That means the captured at Uumshlagplatz have already been counted. So you will have to catch another child on your way to replace your daughter, in order that the Germans will still have their quota and won't notice anything is amiss."

The unexpected words struck Yisrael like a bludgeon. His hands fell to his sides; his shoulders drooped. He froze in the doorway as if he were paralyzed. Finally he turned around slowly to face his wife and the policeman. With a shaking hand he removed the police cap from his head and the identity papers from his pocket and placed them carefully on the table. He gripped the nearest chair and slowly slid down onto it.

His face was white, bloodless. Hope had been crushed into bleak despair. He felt that the rapid shift from extreme to extreme threatened his sanity. He began to weep. Between sobs, he screamed, "Oy! My precious daughter, my beloved only child — No! No, I cannot. I must not, my daughter. Only you am I permitted to sacrifice. Not someone else's. Only mine. Only from my own...."

Source: Translated-adapted by Yerachmiel Tilles from the Hebrew weekly *Sichat HaShavua*, #364. (First published on chabad.org, in 5762/2002)

A Reserved Chair 28

Biographical notes for this story:

Rabbi **Yosef Yitzchak Schneersohn** [of blessed memory: 12 Tammuz 5640– 10 Shvat 5710 (Jan. 1880– June 1950 C.E.)], known as the ***Rebbe Rayatz***, was the sixth Lubavitcher Rebbe, from 5680 to 5710 (1920–1950 C.E.). He established a network of Jewish educational institutions and chasidim that was the single most significant factor for the preservation of Judaism during the dread reign of the Communist Soviets. In 5700 (1940 C.E.) he moved to the USA, established the Chabad world-wide headquarters in Brooklyn, and launched the global campaign to renew and spread Judaism in all languages and in every corner of the world. The campaign continued and was expanded upon remarkably successfully by his son-in-law and successor (see next).

The Lubavitcher Rebbe, Rabbi **Menachem Mendel Schneerson** ז"ן [11 Nissan 5662– 3 Tammuz 5754 (April 1902– June 1994 C.E.), became the seventh Rebbe of the Chabad dynasty after his father-in-law's passing on 10 Shvat 5710 (1950 C.E.). See further biography notes with stories 30 and 33.

This story can be related to:

Weekly Readings: *Miketz* — Genesis ch. 41:40 ("...Only in the chair will I be greater than you" — i.e. I will not give it to you.)

Jewish Calendar Date: *Shvat* 10 (5 days before *Tu b'Shvat*) — *yahrzeit* of Rabbi Y. Y. Shneersohn of Lubavitch; *Shvat* 11 5710 — official assumption of leadership by his son-in-law, Rabbi M. M. Shneerson.

Themes: Rebbe-chasid, Divine Providence, Synagogues, Bronx

A Reserved Chair

One day in 5717 (1957 c.e.), Michel Vishetsky was making the rounds of the synagogues to raise money for *Ezras Achim*, (an American organization which sent food packages to Jews in Russia). He entered a shul in the Bronx, and the only person on the premises was an old Jew, who was sitting off to the side, immersed in a volume of Talmud. He turned out to be **Rabbi Rabinowitz**, the rabbi of the shul. When R. Michel asked to speak to him, the Rabbi led him to a table that he explained was used for the third Shabbos meal.

The Rabbi sat down on a chair along the side of the table. When Reb Michel happened to sit at the head of the table in order to sit near him, the Rabbi jumped up and asked Reb Michel to please move to another chair. "No one may sit in that chair!" the elderly man exclaimed.

"Why is that?" asked the curious chasid.

"It is a long story, but if you have time, I am happy to tell you," said the Rabbi.

"I am from Poland, from a chasidic family. When World War II broke out, I managed to escape across the Russian border. There I fell in with a large group of Chabad chasidim who were headed for Samarkand in Buchara. When I saw the great sacrifices they made for Torah and mizvot, I became very close to them with all my heart and soul.

"When the war ended, I flitted from one place to another. Eventually, in 1949, I arrived in New York.

"Since I had heard so much from those Russian chasidim about Rabbi **Yosef Yitzchak of Lubavitch**, I wanted to visit him. When I was able to enter for *yechidus* (private audience) and mentioned to the Rebbe about my war experiences, the Rebbe asked me many questions about the situation of the chasidim I had met. When I related to him the hardship and suffering I had witnessed, he started to cry in front of me.

"After that, the Rebbe asked me about my plans. 'I have always been a rabbi,' I answered him, 'but here in America nobody seems to need a European-style rabbi, so I will probably take a factory job.'

"'No,' the Rebbe said to me firmly, 'You must remain in a Torah framework. You should continue to serve as a rabbi.'

"I accepted his holy advice and began to look for a rabbinic position. I was unable to find anything. I went back to the Rebbe and reported my lack of success, but he insisted that I be determined and continue to search. Finally, in mid-winter, I discovered this shul. The members all spoke Yiddish. They seemed to like me and decided to offer me the position.

"I traveled back to Brooklyn to consult the Rebbe if I should accept. He gave me a strange reply: 'A shul is a shul, but I don't care for the *shammash (*manager of the shul),' were his words.

"I asked him again what I should do, but the Rebbe only repeated his words. I couldn't understand so I asked him a third time, but the reply was the same thing. Finally he agreed for me to accept the offer.

"After I started the job and was there a while, I found out the meaning of the Rebbe's previously incomprehensible statement. The shammash had a long beard and an impressive appearance, but I quickly discovered that his behavior did not measure up. Then, once, when Shabbos had already begun, I found him lighting candles in the shul! I screamed at him. After that, he seemed to devote himself to making trouble for me, both in shul procedures and with the congregants. He soon succeeded in turning a significant percentage of them against me.

"After a while, I felt I couldn't tolerate it any more. I went to see the Rebbe, this time asking his permission to quit. 'No,' he replied, 'Didn't I tell you: A shul is a shul, but I don't care for the shammash. Don't leave.'

"The situation continued to worsen. The shammash succeeded in making my life even more miserable. Once more I ran back to the Rebbe. 'G-d will help,' he assured me. 'Remember a shul is a shul, with everything that belongs to it.'

"As I was leaving, the Rebbe called to me at the door, 'Also, you should come here Sunday morning.'

"I didn't know why he had said that, but I came that Sunday anyway. A huge funeral was taking place. The day before, on Shabbos, the 10th of Shvat 5710 (1950), the Rebbe passed away. Then I understood: he knew I would want to be there.

"A year passed, but the situation remained oppressive. I heard that the Rebbe Rayatz's younger son-in-law had accepted to be the next Rebbe, so I went to visit him and told him my problem. To my surprise, as soon as I finished speaking he responded, 'Isn't it so that my father-in-law told you that a shul is a shul and he didn't care for the shammash?'

"I was stunned speechless. How did he know?

"The Rebbe continued. 'This means that he can't remain the shammash, because my father-in-law doesn't approve!'

"'But,' I interjected, 'it is not within my authority to fire him.'

"'*Nu*. When you catch him doing something wrong,' smiled the Rebbe, 'then you can have him dismissed.'

"I left the Rebbe's office and returned to the Bronx. The next morning, on the way to the shul, I encountered one of the congregational leaders. I was somewhat surprised, as he was not in the habit of coming early to the weekday minyan as I was.

"We entered the shul together, and were greeted with a shocking sight. There was the shammash, emptying all of the contents of the different *tzedakah* boxes into his pocket.

Caught red-handed by an important member of the shul in addition to me, none of his machinations could help him. He was summarily dismissed from the job.

"Several years passed, andthe shul flourished, but then, a new problem arose.

Years before, there had been a butcher shop next to the shul, sharing a common wall. Its owner prospered, and decided to move the store to larger premises across the street. He offered to sell his old shop to the shul, and the board of directors were happy to agree. They were now able to expand the shul, which had become seriously overcrowded. For certain reasons, however, a contract was never signed even though the butcher was paid.

"One day, all of a sudden, the owner of the butcher shop came and demanded that the shul return his property to him. His business was expanding and he wanted the space back to use for a warehouse, he claimed. He had never sold it to us, but only allowed us to use it. We were shocked, but had no proof that we had bought it. He took us to court and, of course, he won, since the deed was still registered in his name.

"After the official verdict, we were served with an eviction notice. I hurried to Brooklyn, to the Rebbe, and asked him what we should do. The Rebbe looked at me, smiled and said, 'It seems that you are not a chasid, Rabbi Rabinowitz. My revered father-in-law said that a shul is a shul with everything that belongs to it. It is not possible to turn a shul into a butcher shop!'

"I left, perplexed but hopeful.

The night before the court decision was to be executed, and the shul evicted, I had a dream. I saw the Rebbe, Rabbi Yosef Yitzchak, of blessed memory, sitting at the head of *this* table. Standing next to him was the present Rebbe. Rabbi Yosef Yitzchak was smiling at me with a shining face and saying 'A shul is a shul. It will never turn into a butcher shop.'

"I woke up suddenly in confusion and was shocked to

discover that it was already eight o'clock! I was always at shul by six o'clock in the morning.

"I raced to shul as fast as I could. A frenetic, distressing scene was already taking place. Policemen were dragging benches out of the shul onto the street. A large crowd had gathered to stare.

"Suddenly we heard the wail of an ambulance. It stopped right outside the butcher shop across the street. Many of us went over to see what was going on. I went in, and there was the owner, stretched out on the ground, unconscious and bleeding. A large crossbeam had somehow become dislodged from the ceiling and fallen right on his head.

"The men from the ambulance placed him on a stretcher. Just then, he opened his eyes. His gaze found me and he cried out, 'Rabbi! Save me! I admit it! I did sell you my old shop. I did receive full payment. Tell the police to leave the shul alone.'

"Many witnesses heard his confession besides the Rabbi. The eviction was halted."

Rabbi Rabinowitz concluded his astonishing story to a, by then, deeply moved chasid: "From then on, *nobody* sits on that chair at the head of the table. That is the chair in my dream on which the Rebbe, Rabbi Yosef Yitzchak of blessed memory, sat."

Source: Translated-adapted by Yerachmiel Tilles from the Hebrew weekly *Sichat HaShavua*, #263. (First published in Kfar Chabad Magazine — English, in 5758/1997.) Subsequently supplemented with a few details from the Vishetsky family.

Rotten Seeds 29

Biographical note for this story:

Rabbi **Benyamin** (ben Menachem Mendel) **Mendelson,** of blessed memory: ?– 24 Iyar 5739 (?– May 1979 C.E.)] was born in Plotzk, Poland. He immigrated to Israel after WWII, where he became the founding rabbi of Komemiyut, a religious moshav in the south, which, under his guidance and rabbinical leadership, became one of the first settlements to observe *all* the biblical and rabbinical agricultural laws which apply to the Holy Land. He is still considered a foremost authority on the laws of the Sabbatical Year.

This story can be related to:

Weekly Readings: *Bahar* — Leviticus Ch. 25 ("The Sabbatical Year")

Jewish Calendar Date: the next Sabbatical year begins Rosh Hashana 5775 (Sept. 2014 C.E.)

Main Themes: Sabbatical year

Other Topics: Israel, Moshavim and kibbutzim, Farming, Divine supervision

Rotten Seeds

My name is Dov Weiss and I was one of a group of about thirty religious young men that started *Moshav Komemiyut*, an agricultural settlement in the south of Israel. It was in 1950, after we had completed our army service. I was still a bachelor then. Among the founders was also the well known Torah scholar and rabbinical authority, Rabbi **Benyamin Mendelson**, of blessed memory. He had immigrated to Israel from Poland and had served as the Rabbi of Kfar Ata.

At first we lived in tents, in the middle of a barren wilderness. The nearest settlements to ours were several kibbutzim associated with the left-wing *Shomer Hatzair* movement: Gat, Gilon, and Negvah. Several of our members supported themselves by working at Kibbutz Gat, the closest to us, doing different types of manual labor. Others worked in our fields, planting wheat, barley, rye and other grains and legumes. I myself drove a tractor. We sold our produce, which grew throughout the 15,000 or so *dunam* [nearly 4,000 acres] allotted us, to bakeries and factories.

At that time, there were no water pipes reaching our *moshav*. We had to content ourselves with what could be grown in dry rugged fields. Every few days we would make a trip to Kibbutz Negvah, about 20 kilometers away, to fill large containers with drinking water.

The second year we were there, 5711 on the Jewish calendar (Fall 1950– Summer 1951 C.E.) was the *Shmitah* year which comes every seventh year, in which the Torah commands us to desist from all agricultural work (see Leviticus 25:1–7). We were among the very few settlements in Israel at the time to observe the laws of the Sabbatical year, and refrain from working the land. Instead, we concentrated on building, and succeeded that year in completing much of the permanent housing. The moshav gradually developed and expanded, and more and more families moved in, as well as a number of young singles. By the end of the year, we already numbered around eighty people.

As the Sabbatical year drew to its completion, we prepared to renew our farming activities. For this we required seeds to sow crops, but for this purpose we could only use wheat from the sixth year, the year that preceded the *Shmitah*, for the produce of the Seventh Year is forbidden for this type of use. We went around to all the agricultural settlements in the area, near and far, seeking good quality seeds from the previous year's harvest, but no one could fulfill our request.

All we were able to find was some old wormy seed that, for reasons that were never made clear to us, was laying around in a storage shed in Kibbutz Gat. No farmer in his right mind anywhere in the world would consider using such poor quality seed to plant with if he expected to see any crops from it. The kibbutzniks at Gat all burst into loud derisive laughter when we revealed that we were actually interested in this infested grain that had been rotting away for a few years in some dark, murky corner.

"If you really want it, you can take all that you like, and for free, with our compliments," they offered in amusement.

We consulted with Rabbi Mendelson. His response was: "Take it. The One who tells wheat to sprout from good seed can also order it to grow from inferior wormy leftover seed as well."

In any case, we didn't have an alternative. So we loaded a tractor with all the old infested seed that the kibbutz had offered to us free of charge and returned to Komemiyut.

The laws of *Shmitah* forbade us to plough and turn over the soil until after *Rosh HaShana*, the beginning of the eighth year, so we didn't get to actually sow the seed until the next month, *Mar'cheshvan*. This was two or three months after all the other farmers had already completed their planting.

That year, the rains were late in coming. The farmers from all the kibbutzim and moshavim gazed upward longingly for the first rain. They began to feel desperate, but the heavens were unresponsive, remaining breathlessly still and blue.

Finally it rained. When? The day after we completed planting our thousand dunam of wheat fields with those wormy seeds, the sky opened up and the rains exploded down to saturate the parched earth.

The following days we were nervous in anticipation, but we turned our attention to strengthening our faith and trust in G-d. Anyway, it did not take a long time for the hand of the Al-mighty to be revealed clearly to all. Those wheat fields that were planted during the Seventh Year, months before the first rain, sprouted only small weak crops. At the same time, our fields, sowed with the old infested seed and long after the optimal time, were covered with an unusually large and healthy yield of wheat, in comparison to any standard.

The story of the "miracle at Komemiyut" spread quickly. Farmers from all the agricultural settlements in the south came to see with their own eyes what they could not believe when they heard the rumors about it.

When the farmers from Kibbutz Gat arrived, they pulled a surprise on us. After looking in open-mouthed astonishment at the impressive bountiful quantity of wheat flourishing in our fields, grown from the infested seeds they had provided us, they decided to renege on their generosity. They announced they wanted payment for the tractor load of old rotten wheat they had scornfully given us for free only a short time before.

Even more startling: they said they would file a claim against us at the *beit din* (rabbinical court), and with Rabbi Mendelson himself, no less! They figured that in a secular court such a claim wouldn't have the slightest possible chance of gaining them even a single penny.

Rabbi Mendelson accepted their case seriously, and in the end judged that we should pay them. His explained that the reason they gave it for free was because they thought it worthless for planting, while in truth it really was excellent for that purpose. We were astonished to hear his ruling, but needless to say, we complied.

The whole story became an extraordinary *kiddush Hashem* (glorification of G-d), in the eyes of people throughout the country. Everyone agreed it was a clear fulfillment of G-d's promise in the Torah:

> *If you shall say, "What shall we eat in the seventh year? Behold we shall not plant, nor harvest our produce!" I will command my blessing to you...." [Leviticus 25:20–21].*

Source: Translated and freely adapted by Yerachmiel Tilles from the Hebrew weekly *Sichat HaShavua*, #721. (First published on *AscentOf Safed. com.)*

Translator's note:

—

In addition to being a leader in the observance of the agricultural commandments that apply in the Land of Israel, **Komemiyut** is world famous for its high-quality (and tasty!) *shmurah matzah* — round, hand-made matzah prepared under exacting supervision from the time the wheat is harvested through to the end of the baking, guarding the wheat and the matzah against the minutest moisture.

The Tenth Man

Biographical notes:

The Lubavitcher Rebbe, Rabbi **Menachem Mendel Schneerson** נ"ע [11 Nissan 5662– 3 Tammuz 5754 (April 1902– June 1994 C.E.), became the seventh Rebbe of the Chabad dynasty after his father-in-law's passing on 10 Shvat 5710 (1950 C.E.). He is widely acknowledged as the greatest Jewish leader of the second half of the 20th Century. Although a dominant scholar in both the revealed and hidden aspects of Torah, and fluent in many languages and scientific subjects, the Rebbe is best known for his extraordinary love and concern for every Jew on the planet. His emissaries around the globe, dedicated to strengthening Judaism, number in the thousands. Hundreds of volumes of his teachings have been printed, as well as many dozens of English translations.

This story can be related to:

Weekly Readings: *Bechukotai* — Leviticus 25:32 ("...The tenth one [counted] shall be holy.")

Jewish Calendar Date: *Nissan* 11 (four days before Pesach) — birth date of the Lubavitcher Rebbe; *Tammuz* 3 (two weeks before Fast of the 17th) — his *yahrzeit*.

Main Themes: Birthing, Healing, Hidden tzadikim

Other Topics: Israel, Moshavim and kibbutzim, West Coast USA

The Tenth Man

On a certain religious *moshav* in Israel lived a woman who suffered greatly and had health problems whenever she gave birth. With each birth the situation worsened, until finally the doctors told her that she would be endangering her life if she tried to give birth another time, and now she was pregnant again!

She visited great rabbis for advice, and kabbalists and chasidic rebbes for blessings. She also prayed at the gravesites of the many righteous ones buried in the Holy Land. Nevertheless, she still felt frightened, as recent examinations had not revealed any change for the better in her condition. Then, someone suggested to her that she write to the Lubavitcher Rebbe in Brooklyn. It seemed strange and a bit silly to her to consult someone outside of Israel, but she decided to do it. Shortly before she was due to give birth, she received a most remarkable response from the Rebbe.

He wrote that near the moshav in a certain direction was a spring, and on the other side of the spring was a factory. The workers leave there each afternoon at 4:30. Her husband should walk over there before that hour, and stand near the gate. When the workers emerge, he should count them one by one. When the tenth one exited, he should follow him.

What an answer! They could scarcely believe it. Nevertheless, the next day the woman's husband followed the directions, and upon arriving at the factory on the far side of the spring, he took up his post outside the gate. He stared and stared at his watch. Finally it was 4:30. The workers began to file out. 1–2–3.... The tenth man was very ordinary looking. Nothing about him seemed special at all. Indeed, he seemed hardly distinguishable from the ones before him or after him. The husband shrugged. The Rebbe said to follow him, so follow him he would.

The man walked and walked, finally arriving at a nearby settlement. He went straight to a certain house, entered and closed the door behind him, just as anyone would do upon returning home from a day on the job. The husband stood gazing from a distance, momentarily perplexed, but then realized he had no choice other than to try to enter the house after him.

He approached the house and knocked on the door. A woman opened the door and asked him what he wanted. He told her that he wished to speak to the man who had come just before him ... the man who worked at the factory near the spring. The woman nodded and told him to wait. She disappeared inside, and then a few minutes later, the man he had followed came to the door.

The man asked his unexpected visitor who he was and why he wished to speak with him. The wide-eyed husband stammered for a moment and then replied, "To tell you the truth I don't know why, but my wife is in a life-threatening situation, and the Lubavitcher Rebbe in New York wrote to us that I should follow you and..."

"I can't believe it!" the man exclaimed, as waves of surprise and emotion passed over his face. "Even here the holy rebbe has found me!" He asked his startled visitor to tell him the whole story.

The husband related about his wife's difficulties each time she gave birth, their letter to the Rebbe, and the strange answer they had received. "So I went to the factory and you were the tenth man. I followed you here, as the Rebbe directed, but more than that I do not know."

The man smiled. "Just wait right here a few moments," he said resignedly. He went back inside the house and shortly afterwards returned, displaying a few sugar cubes in his hand.

"These are for your wife," he said, but then, much to the husband's surprise, he added, "But not for *this* birth.

"That's because she already gave birth, just a few seconds ago! She and the baby are both healthy, *Baruch Hashem*; there were no problems at all."

The husband was speechless. He wanted so much for the words he was hearing to be true, but he didn't know if he could safely believe them or not.

The man continued, "These sugar cubes are for future births. If she has any problems, give her these sugar cubes to eat and everything will be fine right away."

The husband bubbled over with profuse thanks, and the two men parted warmly. When he reached the moshav, he quickly discovered that his wife had indeed given birth, with no complications, and exactly when the mystery man had said.

All the residents of the moshav rejoiced at the good news of the unexpectedly smooth birth, and even more so when they heard the extraordinary accompanying story. A few of them set out to get a blessing or a word of advice or just to glimpse the secret holy man, but they were not able to find him. The house was vacant and he no longer worked at the factory.

Source: The first part of this story is translated and adapted by Yerachmiel Tilles from *Sipurei Chasidim L'noar*—vol.2, based on an article in *Kfar Chabad Magazine*. (First published on *AscentOf Safed. com.*)

Translator's note:

—

This story is known to us from a non-Lubavitcher chasid who, at the time of the episode, was living on the moshav, and heard it first-hand from the couple. Who the "tenth man" was, or where he is now, I cannot tell you, but we may have caught a trace of him here at Ascent in Safed!

A few years ago, during an Ascent Shabbat meal, a student from the (non-chasidic) Torah VaDaas Yeshiva in Brooklyn stood up and asked permission to tell a story about the Lubavitcher Rebbe. He testified that he heard the story from his brother-in-law, who heard it from his study partner at the (non-chasidic) Chaim Berlin Yeshiva Kollel in Brooklyn, to whom it happened. It turned out to be nearly the exact same story I just told you, including the difficulty in giving birth, the surprise of the hidden holy man at being discovered, and the sugar cubes. However, instead of a moshav, a spring, a factory and counting to ten, there was a remote location on the Northwest coast of the USA, which entailed a plane, and a bus, and a taxi to get there. Also, in this version the husband delivered the sugar cubes to his wife just in time before the birth to ease the difficulties. And instead of others, the husband himself made the trip again to thank the benefactor, but he was no longer there. When he reported this back to the Rebbe, the Rebbe just smiled.

Don't Be Surprised

Biographical notes:

Rabbi **Aharon Yechiel Leifer,** of blessed memory: ?– 1 Sivan 5760 (?– June 2000 C.E.), was born in Bania, Rumania, where his father, Dovid, served as Rebbe, a descendent of the famous Galitzean dynasty of Nodvorna rebbes. As a young man he served as the Rabbi of Shatz, his wife's birthplace, also in Rumania. He arrived in Israel shortly after the war of Liberation in 1948. Previously he had lost an entire family in the Holocaust, but had married his deceased wife's sister and started a whole new family. Legendary in Tzefat for his hospitality and kindness to those in need, his home and shul were a center for Jews of all stripes for fifty-two years. Beloved equally by chasidim, Sephardim and Ashkenazism, by Europeans, Israelis and Americans, his death at the age of about ninety marked the end of an era in Tzefat.

This story can be related to:

Weekly Readings: *Shoftim* — Deuteronomy 17:9–10 ("You shall come to the Kohanim, the Levite and the judge who will be in those times ... you shall be careful to do according to everything that they tell you.")

The Jewish Holidays: *Rosh Hodesh Sivan* (see next line)

Jewish Calendar Date: *Sivan* 1 (five days before *Shavuot*) — *yahrzeit* of the Nadvorna Rebbe of Tzefat.

Main Themes: Matchmaking

Other Topics: Tzefat, *Aliyah*, Faith in Rebbes

Don't Be Surprised

SHORTLY BEFORE PASSOVER in 1995, when Dr. Rafael Rosen got married to his wife Adina, , an old friend of his from the States attended his wedding. Noah Betterman was also a medical practitioner, an acupuncturist, who was visiting Israel at the time. When he first came he didn't know about his friend's nuptial plans, but when he found out, he was happy to participate in the celebration.

Rosh Chodesh Sivan is the yahrzeit of Rabbi ***Aharon Yechiel Leifer, the Nadvorner-Bania Rebbe of Zefat.*** *At the first yahrzeit minyan in 2001, a friend of mine, a doctor and healer whom Rabbi Leifer had influenced fifteen years before to sell his medical practice in Oklahoma and make aliyah, told me this story about his Rebbe.*

At the wedding, Noah had the opportunity to meet Rabbi Leifer. He was very impressed, but regretted not being able to communicate with him, as he spoke neither Hebrew or Yiddish (or Romanian or Hungarian). With only a few days remaining on his trip before he had to fly back, he asked Rafael to arrange a meeting with the Rebbe for him and to act as a translator.

On Shabbat HaGadol, after the *kiddush* featuring Rebbetzen Leifer's world-famous cholent, the three sat down together. When Rabbi Leifer heard about Noah's travel plans, he immediately told him to delay his departure. When Noah shrugged his inability, the Rebbe insisted, telling him it would be beneficial for him both in matters of health and in finding his soulmate. Noah began listing the reasons why he *had to* return: work obligations, *seder* commitments, a sick uncle, etc. To his surprise, Dr. Rosen refused to translate his protests, saying that either Noah would heed the Rebbe's advice or not, as he chose, but by no means would he help him to oppose the Rebbe's words. The Rebbe blessed Noah, who left with his plans unchanged, content.

Man proposed, G-d disposes, as they say. Just a day or two before his scheduled departure, Noah became seriously sick, so much so that he had to cancel his flight. He remained in Jerusalem for Passover, and there he encountered Tamar, someone he had met previously. Their relationship deepened and they agreed to seriously pursue the possibility of marriage. They both returned to the States, which constituted no obstacle, as he lived in Berkeley California at the time and she in San Francisco, just across the Bay!

Shortly thereafter they married, and having decided to begin their life together in the Holy Land, moved to Israel and eventually ended up in Tzefat. The following Shabbat HaGadol, Noah went to speak to Rabbi Leifer again. By this time he was able to manage in Hebrew by himself, without a translator. He related to the Rebbe the story of all that had transpired over the course of the year, and expressed his amazement and delight at the series of seeming coincidences that had so quickly and dramatically altered his life.

"But you had a blessing," Rabbi Leifer responded offhandedly. "Why are you so surprised?"

Source: Written by Yerachmiel Tilles, based on his conversation with Dr. Rafael Rosen. (First published on *AscentOf Safed. com.*)

Slaps Of Love 32

Biographical notes for this story:

Rabbi **Moshe Weber,** [of blessed memory: 5 Kislev 5675– 18 Adar-a 5760 (1914– March 2000 C.E.)] was a central and beloved figure in Jerusalem's religious community. Nearly every day he went to the Western Wall from his home in Meah Shearim to pray and to help visitors wrap tefillin. Less publicly, he distributed enormous sums of *tzedakah*(charity) to the city's poor. It is known that, decades before, the *Lubavitcher Rebbe* said of him that he was one of the holiest and kindest people in the world. He published several volumes of Torah insights in *Yarim Moshe*. There is an ongoing periodical of his teachings distributed weekly called *Shemu V'Techi Nafshechem*, which also offers his audio recordings in Hebrew for sale.

This story can be related to:

Weekly Readings: *Kedoshim* — Leviticus 19:18 ("You must love your fellow [Jew] as [you love] yourself." — Rabbi Akiva: "This is the major principle of the Torah.")

Jewish Calendar Date: *Adar-a* 18 (4 days after Purim in a regular (non-leap) year) — *yahrzeit* of Rabbi Moshe Weber

Main Themes: Conversion

Other Topics: Israel, Jerusalem, Tzefat, Marriage, Love

Slaps Of Love

Two Americans are visiting Israel. It is January 1988, just after the beginning of the Intifada. They had met as secular people, business people, working in the same city. Their relationship had developed over a year's time to include concerts, restaurants, lectures, and ever-intensifying discussions concerning religion. Although nontraditional in almost every way you can imagine, they were trying to sort out their lives, and just beginning to learn about Torah Judaism.

The elder, an American businessman in his 40's, arrived in Jerusalem in November 1987 and began taking classes at different beginners' yeshivas for English-speakers. The woman, in her late twenties at the time, arrived January 1. She had just quit her job suddenly, sold most of her belongings, and stored the rest. She felt she was embarking on a whole new path on her life's journey. Her intent was to meet up with this man, see some of Israel with him, and discuss her decision about Judaism.

Although she had grown up orthodox Protestant, she had found Judaism at the end of her college career. Her apartment was lined with books, including translations of biblical texts and a tome on Jewish Law. The real truth was that she knew more about Judaism than he had from day one!

When he left for Israel to learn, they had parted ways but expected to remain friends. Three weeks into the separation, she was picking up the phone to call his daughter and get a telephone number to reach him when the phone rang. When she heard his voice again, she knew. She would go to Israel. What happened after that was up to G-d. Little did she know!

One afternoon, a tour guide took them to see Meah Shaarim, the most strictly religious Jewish neighborhood in the world. The weather was very cold and wet, a virtual deluge. The narrow streets were dark and full of water runoff.

The guide showed them the basics and then, with a wink, announced that he had a brilliant idea, something off the beaten track. As he led them through slippery alleys, occasionally cutting between ramshackle buildings, he explained that he was taking them to visit an old friend. He did not say a tzadik. These two would not have known a tzadik unless hit between the eyes with one ... which is precisely what happened next!

Knocking on a little door, they were met by a very tall, broad-shouldered, red-haired young man and a very short, bent, frail-looking older man, apparently on their way out. Both were dressed in traditional Jerusalem chasidic garb. Later, the couple found out that the older man had been about to go to the shul where he conducted a daily class in *Daf Yomi* [a two-sided page of Talmud per day].

The young man motioned them in. The Rabbi greeted them in what the man recognized as Yiddish. He had heard his grandmother speak the language many, many years before. The woman had no clue what was going on, but the look of kindness on the little old man's face and the intensity of his eyes made her knees weak and her heart open.

Introductions were made. The young man was Ido Erhlich, close disciple and constant companion to the elder one, **Rabbi Moshe Weber**, and his translator into English for innocents such as they who knew neither Hebrew or Yiddish.

Although Rabbi Weber did not know a word of English, he still knew how to communicate quite effectively. He held the man's right hand affectionately between both of his for a number of moments, and then motioned for the two of them to sit down at the table. He started to speak to them excitedly about Israel, Torah, and mitzvot. They couldn't understand a word, but nevertheless glowed at the obvious warmth and caring that was expressed in the tone of his voice and his kind sparkling eyes. They were thankful that Ido was present and able to act as a translator.

But then, in the tiny, dim, eight by eight room, the visiting couple's lives were transformed before the light of one tiny candle on the small gray formica table.

Rabbi Weber seated them at the table, asked if they would like something to drink or eat, and sent Ido for some cookies. After gently instructing him to say the proper blessings, Rabbi Weber took the hands of the gentleman between his and spoke calmly but urgently to him; every once in a while he would gently slap one of the man's cheeks. Apparently he was suggesting that his guest discontinue the use of his razor. If he had to shave, he could buy an electric shaver when he returned to the U.S.

After a few minutes, the man revealed that the woman accompanying him was not Jewish and that it was his intention to marry her. When he said that, Ido seemed shocked, and upset. Perhaps he thought that Rabbi Weber should either yell at the man for daring to bring a non-Jewish woman into his house and for brazenly announcing his plans to intermarry, or more simply, immediately ask the two of them to leave.

Rabbi Weber did neither. He continued to speak to the man in warm friendly tones and in a heartfelt manner, stressing the beauty and fulfillment in a life based on mitzvah observance. Within minutes, the truth of the expression, words that emerge from the heart enter the heart, was visible to all.

Once or twice the Rabbi looked into the eyes of the woman, conferred with Ido and the guide, then suggested that she consider candle lighting — not that she should actually light... yet, but that she should consider the light of the Shabbat candles. At this time, Mrs. Weber was very ill, but she was ushered in to her, introduced, and given a seat next to her bed. Of course neither one could speak the other's language, but they managed to communicate on some level.

The male visitor was obviously affected by the warmth and love with which Rabbi Weber was speaking to him. He declared that he was ready* to commit himself to putting on tefillin every weekday and to keeping Shabbat.

[**His recent intense four days at Ascent in Zefat helped prepare him for this.* —Y.T.]

"Very good," replied Rabbi Weber, "but that is not sufficient. You must know that it is forbidden for you to be with this woman!"

Actually, no one had said outright what was the relationship between the two. Still, it was obvious that the rabbi had sized the situation up very quickly.

The man quickly responded that it was her intention to convert, and had been so for a long time, even before she had met him. Rabbi Weber answered him that if it was indeed her desire to join the Jewish people and accept the yoke of Torah and Mitzvot, she would have to do so under the auspices of an Orthodox rabbi in the city where she lived in the USA.

They promised that was exactly what would happen. The man parted from Rabbi Weber with a warm hug, and a promise that he would do precisely as the rabbi had instructed him.

After that wet evening, when the sun came out the next morning, everything looked different. They were amazed that Rabbi Weber had taken the time to speak with two such misfit American unknowns, help the man make blessings, and urge him towards doing more mitzvot: tefillin, prayer, and Shabbat. A whole shul packed with his students was kept waiting on account of these two. They felt humbled, honored, confused, and elated all at once, as if a vision of their whole future together had just unrolled before them.

She had made the commitment to an orthodox conversion long before, but he had not been sure what that would mean for him, and the necessity for his parallel commitment to a Torah life: *Shabbat, mikveh, kashrut*—you know, the whole 613. Now it was clear. They were to lead an observant life together, even with the many years between their chronological ages, and even with her 20 years of diabetes behind her and an uncertain future ahead.

A half-year went by. One day, Rabbi Weber received an overseas phone call. It was that same American Jew. Rabbi Weber beckoned to Ido to take the receiver.

The American said that the woman had undergone a strictly kosher conversion, and that he had increased his personal level of observance as he had promised Rabbi Weber. He then announced that they were planning to marry soon, and they both deeply wished that Rabbi Weber would accept their invitation to attend their wedding in Pittsburgh, which they would send formally as soon as the date was set.

Rabbi Weber explained to him through Ido that such a long trip would be impossible for him, as his wife was seriously ill and bedridden, and he had to be available to care for her. "But Reb Moshe," the man exclaimed, "you must come. We both desperately want you to be there. We need you to come. *And you asked us to invite you!*"

He was referring to the incident just before they left Israel, when they had visited in Meah Shaarim once more. Rabbi Weber, through Ido, had asked the man to please make sure the woman did her learning with Chabad ... and to be sure to invite him to speak at the wedding! The gentleman had marveled at this, but now he had a much better appreciation of the tzadik, and since Rabbi Weber had asked him to do this, he made sure to do it!

The date for the wedding suddenly had to be advanced. The father of the *kallah* (bride) had become very ill. It was rescheduled for *Chai Elul*, a special day among the chasidim [which falls at the end of summer, 12 days before Rosh Hashana]. With very little notice, invitations were quickly designed, calligraphy-addressed, and mailed. There were to be eighty friends and family around the wedding canopy.

Ido telephoned. The invitation had taken only 4 days to

arrive at the Webers—from the U.S. to Israel, to Mea Shaarim in just four days! A miracle. And that summer, Mrs. Weber was admitted to a special rehabilitation home, for which she had been on a waiting list for many months! Another miracle!

"We can come," Ido told them excitedly." They, of course, were thrilled.

The joy of that unique wedding was extraordinary. Rabbi Weber danced with the *chatan* (bridegroom) for a long time. Everyone present was enthralled and delighted by the special guest from Jerusalem. It is now more than a decade later, and they still speak about it.

The Creator provides in abundance! Not only were Ido and Rabbi Weber able to come to the wedding, they spent all of the holidays from Rosh HaShanah through Simchat Torah with the Lubavitcher Rebbe . It was the first time in thirty years Rabbi Weber had left the Land of Israel!

Thirteen months after the wedding, the new couple visited Rabbi Weber again, this time with an infant son, during Sukkot. They continued to be supporters of his work and spoke with Ido frequently, exchanging messages with the Rabbi. He served as a guiding vision in their lives until his passing in 2000.

The couple subsequently moved to San Diego, California, where they established a true Jewish home. They had three sons, all of whom grew to study in fine Torah institutions. Every Shabbat, they invite many guests, some of whom they help draw closer to Torah-true Judaism. During the week they also host observant Jews from different communities who are visiting their city.

Who knows? Perhaps the reason Rabbi Weber was so patient with them at their first encounter, at his house, was simply an outcome of his kind and caring nature. Ido declares it was because he saw with true vision the potential for the fine Jewish home that would emerge from their union.

The Morrows, Reuven and I, Sara-Chana, who has been

relating to you our story in third person, hold our memories of Rabbi Weber dear to our hearts, and keep his memory alive by teaching our three sons, and sharing with our guests, the many lessons we learned at that little table by the light of that one tiny candle, light that illuminated a world full of Torah, kindness to others, effervescent joy, and considerate behavior.

Source: Translated and retold by Yerachmiel Tilles from an article in *Shemu V'techi Nafshechem* (#309) by Rabbi Yitzchak Ido Weber-Erhlich, but primarily based on personal acquaintance with all the characters mentioned, and on a detailed letter from Mrs. Morrow.] (An earlier version was first published on *AscentOf Safed. com*, but was extensively revised for this book.)

Author's note:

—

Rabbi Weber was "*sandek sheini*" and guest speaker at the *brit mila* of my youngest son in 5748/1988 C.E. Yosef repaid him by having his first child on **18 Adar-a** 5771/2011 C.E.

Biographical notes for this story:

The Lubavitcher Rebbe, Rabbi **Menachem Mendel Schneerson** ז"ל [11 Nissan 5662– 3 Tammuz 5754 (April 1902– June 1994 C.E.)], became the seventh Rebbe of the Chabad dynasty after his father-in-law's passing on 10 Shvat 5710 (1950 C.E.). He is widely acknowledged as the greatest Jewish leader of the second half of the 20th Century. Although a dominant scholar in both the revealed and hidden aspects of Torah and fluent in many languages and scientific subjects, the Rebbe is best known for his extraordinary love and concern for every Jew on the planet. His emissaries around the globe, dedicated to strengthening Judaism, number in the thousands. Hundreds of volumes of his teachings have been printed, as well as dozens of English renditions.

This story can be related to:

Weekly Readings: *Tetzaveh* — Exodus 28:2 ("...garments that are *l'kavod u'l'tiferet* [dignified and beautiful])."

Jewish Calendar Date: *Nissan* 11 (4 days before Pesach) — birth date of the Lubavitcher Rebbe; *Tammuz* 3 (two weeks before Fast of the 17th) — *yahrzeit* of the Lubavitcher Rebbe.

Main Themes: Dreams, Divine supervision

Other Topics: Tefilin, Mitzvah (commandments), Mobile, Neckties, Chasid-Rebbe

Tied Up

I REMEMBER IT AS CLEARLY as if it happened yesterday. It was Tuesday night, after midnight, *Gimmel Adar Aleph* 5749 (March 8, '89) when I had the strangest dream. **The [Lubavitcher] Rebbe** appeared to me. He was smiling, which is a wonderful sign. He addressed me by my first name and said, "Tomorrow you should wear a necktie."

There are other versions of this story extant, but this one is truer—see source notes at end—and, amazingly, more wondrous than the distorted versions.

Now, even in a dream that sounded ridiculous. I'm one of those yeshiva guys who goes with shirttails hanging out, and I can't claim that I put on a fresh clean shirt everyday either. I guess you could call me a bit extreme. And I should put on a necktie. Preposterous!

I thought that in the context of the dream, and even more so when I woke up. When I went around the corner to [the yeshiva at] 770 [Eastern Parkway in Brooklyn] to board the tank, I didn't tell any of the others about the dream. It was too ridiculous, even though the rebbe was in it.

On Fridays, all the yeshiva students scatter from Lubavitch World Headquarters in Brooklyn on the Tefilin Campaign to points all over the city in order to encourage fellow Jewish males to put on tefilin with our help. We also distribute Shabbat candles to Jewish women, and in general do whatever we can to be a helpful Jewish presence. Most travel by subway, but on Wednesdays I also had a route in Manhattan with some other students and we went there in a mitzvah-mobile", or Tefilin Tank, as we liked to call the specially designed mobile-home vans that we used. That Wednesday, as we set out, I briefly remembered the dream and again shook my head in disbelief.

We drove to our usual station on Sixth Avenue and Forty-Second Street, accessible to both the Garment and Diamond districts. I strolled away from the tank a bit and began asking men that looked Jewish if they were indeed Jewish and if they wanted to put on tefilin. A few hours passed and I was thinking about taking a break to get something to eat, when a man with an attaché case walked up to me and addressed me in Yiddish!

It turned out that he was an old Jew from Europe and his attaché case was filled with, of all things, neckties! "Perhaps you want to buy a nice tie?" he asked.

"*Mishigas*" (nonsense), I replied, even though I immediately recalled my dream of the Rebbe the night before. The concept of wearing a tie was still much too foreign. "What would I do with a tie? I've never worn one in my life. Look at me. Do I look like a necktie type of person to you?"

"Still, you should have one," he insisted. "It will go well with your white shirt, and I have a very nice selection."

I shook my head firmly, but at the same time I began to question myself. First the dream and now this? Maybe I really had to consider it.

He continued to urge me and finally I relented. "Okay, I'll look at what you have, but if I am really going to get a tie, which I can't believe, I wouldn't consider anything except what the Rebbe himself wears."

"What's that?" he quickly queried.

"Solid black and 100% pure silk," I told him.

"Oh, I happen to have one like that," he said. "Let me find it for you. "Ah, here it is. As you can see it is of very fine quality. You have good taste. For you, only $80."

I burst into laughter. "You can't be serious! Me, spend $80 on a necktie? Even if I had so much money I wouldn't do it, but of course I don't have. Not even close."

"So how much do you have?

I pulled out all the single dollar bills and loose change from my pockets. A vigorous shaking produced another few nickels and dimes. "A bit over five dollars," I said ruefully.

His eyes opened wide. "Well, in that case, perhaps you would like one of my cheaper samples. They are also very nice."

"No," I said firmly. "Like the Rebbe's, or nothing."

He was silent for a minute, a thoughtful look on his face. "Okay, I'll let you have it for five dollars, but you have to put it on, and wear it too."

I gulped. This was not turning out as I had expected. I never imagined he would give it to me for such a small fraction of his special price. I thought I was rid of him and now I was stuck. "But I can't put it on now. I don't know how," I tried.

"Don't worry," he rejoined. "I'll tie it for you."

I was afraid he would say that. I gave him the money. He counted it carefully and then placed the tie around my neck and under the collar of my shirt. After some mysterious twisting of the two ends he was finished with the knot. He stepped back and said, "Ah. Wonderful. It looks very nice on you. Very becoming. Now you look like a *mentsch*."

I felt like I was choking. I figured that as soon as he went away I would take it off, but it was as if he could read my mind. He insisted that I leave it on for the day and I reluctantly agreed. He smiled, nodded, turned away, and soon disappeared from sight.

Then, something strange happened. I had resumed asking the Jewish-looking men walking by if they would like to put on tefilin, and after a while I noticed that I was getting a much higher percentage of positive responses than usual. "Could it really be the tie?" I wondered to myself. "It just doesn't make sense." Even so, it somehow made an impression, and I accepted that I should probably leave the tie on.

Another hour went by and I had already forgotten I was wearing it. Then it was time to split up and make our rounds of the offices in the vicinity, where a number of the Jewish professionals were used to our weekly appearances. Many even looked forward to our visits.

One exception was the staff of lawyers for a certain law office, which was on my route. Although the non-Jewish lawyers were friendly, and several of the Jewish lawyers were agreeable, the head of the firm never let them take the few minutes to put on tefilin with us. He would complain about wasting time and get upset at whoever let 'those' people in. After a few muttered words to one of his staff he would stalk away, and soon thereafter I would be politely asked to leave. The situation worsened to the point that the reception people were reluctant to buzz me in to enter by the front door, and many times they wouldn't, but I kept trying.

That day, however, they let me in immediately, but as soon as I entered, the first one I encountered, before I could even say hello to the receptionist and the secretaries, was the boss man himself. He gave us a hard stare and said, "You!" in a loud firm tone, and pointed his finger directly at me. "Come with me. Now!"

"Uh oh," I thought. "It finally happened. This lawyer is going to call the police on me or something." But there was no choice. I followed him into his private room.

He closed the door behind us and locked it. I couldn't help noticing how fancy and expensive-looking his office was. He tried making some small talk with me in halting Hebrew. He said that he had been to Hebrew University for a year in his college days. He already was aware that my English wasn't that great. I assured him that I understood much better than I could speak.

He stared at me again. Then he spoke. "I want you to help me put on tefilin," he said quietly, averting his eyes.

Could I believe what just entered my ears? I must have looked stunned, although it probably wasn't difficult for him to figure out how surprised I was. "I am sure you want to know why today I suddenly agreed to let you put tefilin on me. I'll explain afterwards."

I nodded and quickly took the tefilin out of their pouch.

I wrapped them on him and coached him in the blessings and recitation of the *Shma Yisrael* prayer, in which tefilin is mentioned twice. When he finished, I removed the tefilin, returned them to their place, and looked at him expectantly.

He sighed. "I'm sure you see me as a very successful person, but the truth is that I am having a difficult time now. I've been having a number of personal problems, and lately I've been feeling that I could use some aid and advice, but I didn't know where to turn.

"Then, yesterday, I happened to see one of the cards you fellows left here with your rabbi's picture on it, and it struck a chord. I wondered if he could possibly help me.

"Now comes the part that may be difficult for you to believe. Last night I had a dream. I dreamt that I saw the Lubavitcher Rebbe. He smiled and I asked him if he could help me. He answered, 'But I send you a few people every week.' To which I replied, 'What, those slobs? They look like a bunch of vagrants! Who can respect them? Why, none of them even wears a tie!'

"The Rebbe smiled at me again and said 'You want a tie? Okay, I'll send someone with a tie!' And I woke up.

"So when I saw you wearing a tie, I immediately understood that the dream was real. I knew I should put on tefilin with you so I brought you in here. I hope that my situation will now improve."

After that day, he began putting on tefilin on a daily basis, by himself. I saw that his personal and spiritual situation definitely took a turn for the good. Even after I returned to Israel I maintained contact with him. We speak on the phone before every holiday, and whenever I get to New York, we see each other. He seems to be as prosperous as ever, or even more so. Just this winter, eighteen years after this story, he came to Brooklyn to visit me.

By the way, I continued to wear the tie whenever I went on a Tefilin Campaign and I consistently noted increased success. If you are wondering why the other students didn't follow my lead, it is because they never saw me wearing a tie, and I never told them about it. I would put it on only when there were no other fellows around. To be seen wearing a tie? How embarrassing.

Source: Based on the version told to Yerachmiel Tilles in great detail by Y., the main character of the story, who is a resident of Tzefat. (First published on *AscentOf Safed.com*—#500 in the email mailings for the week of 3 Tammuz 5767/2007.)

Acknowledgements

My sincere heartfelt gratitude to the Creator, blessed be He, for allowing and enabling me to reach this point, and to:

The Lubavitcher Rebbe, נ״ד, who breathed life into my Jewish soul.

Meir Abehsera (Abuhatzeira) and his wife Esther, for demonstrating the warmth, beauty and importance of the open Jewish home, and welcoming me into theirs.

Rabbi Akiva Greenberg, who inducted me into the magic of Jewish Saturday Night and chasidic storytelling.

The Rebbe Rayatz and Rabbi S Y. Zevin for modelling important Jewish story-writing principles.

Shaul Y. Leiter, my co-founder (along with Moshe Y. Wisnefsky) and executive director of *Ascent—Inner Dimensions of Jewish Life*, in Tzefat Israel (www.ascentofsafed.com), my second home for the last thirty years and the platform for the honing and mailing of these stories, for his extraordinary efforts and selfless dedication maintaining Ascent for three decades. Let's keep it going until Moshiach and beyond!

The administration and staff of Kfar Chabad Magazine, for the printing of many of these stories during the alas, too-brief existence of their English supplement.

Colleagues Yanki Tauber, Uri Kaploun, and Shterna Citron, who at different points through the years edited some of these stories for their publications.

Chaya-Rachel Benami, my faithful assistant over the years, who continues to find spelling, typing and grammatical mistakes, even though English is my native language and not hers.

Rabbi Alter-Eliyahu ("Elik") Friedman, for reviewing the Saturday night Appendices, and for all the editing and suggestions in the years of *Ascent Quarterly* and *Mother in Israel.*

Eyal Riess and Yahel Dahan of the Ascent Hebrew Seminars, for the "full moon" connection.

Batya Majerczyk for the Table of Contents format inspiration. Morah Yehudis Fishman for ingenius help with some of the Weekly Torah connections.

Rifca-Leah Goldberg for her graphic work for the online preview, and her patience with my endless demands for incremental improvements.

Hershel Robinson, Ascent's techie whiz with a talent for proofreading. Lauren Howitt-Vallone for a sharp suggestion. The people at Menorah Books for valuable advice, fair treatment and professional services: Chaim Natan Firszt — editing, Gal Narunsky — cover graphic and book design, and Ashirah Yosefah — project management.

David Katz Esq., for recommendations on the contract for this book which benefitted both sides.

All those enumerated in the Dedication.

Finally, my nuclear family:

My younger son, Yosef, who encouraged and pestered;

My older son, Yehuda, who vigilantly looks out for stories Abba will like in Hebrew publications;

And of course my wife, Shulamit, who, among her other numerous accomplishments (see the Dedication), single-handedly produced a hardcover forerunner and inspiration for this book eight and a half years ago.

Appendices

a. Saturday Night Live in Judaism

a. THE TIME

Saturday night is a magical time in the Jewish weekly cycle. It is the transition between the holiness and the security of the Shabbat world-onto-itself and the anxious/vulnerable busyness of our weekday involvements. The lingering Shabbat spirit clings, the new week beckons and we feel tugs and reluctances in each direction. On Saturday night our goal is to smoothly consolidate our gains from the Shabbat process, and start to utilize them as a foundation and inspiration for the weekday world that is rushing upon us.

b. THE MEAL

There are many customs associated with Saturday night, and most of them center around the post-Shabbat *meal* (What? Another meal!) that takes place then.

I emphasized "meal" because its mitzvah aspect is dependent on sitting down at a set table, as opposed to, say, snatching a slice of pizza on the run. Candles should be lit (without a blessing) on the table, and there should be something freshly prepared and hot (not just leftovers from Shabbat) for eating and drinking. (*Appendix B: "Some Laws, Customs and Guidelines for the Saturday Night Meal"*)

The chasidic custom is to gather for the Saturday night meal in private homes, not in shul. Still, the meal can be anything from a modest interlude in the privacy of your kitchen nook to an elaborate banquet with hundreds of participants held at a large hall. In well established Jewish communities, many kosher restaurants open Saturday night and feature live entertainment. There is a custom to prepare a dish especially for the Saturday night meal, even if there are plenty of leftovers from Shabbat.

The Talmud (Shabbat 119b) tells us that R. Avahu had a quality calf prepared for him every Saturday night, of which he ate only the kidneys. Thinking it a waste, his son Avimi suggested that he take the kidneys from a calf slaughtered on Friday, cook all the meat for Shabbat, thereby saving another entire animal. R. Avahu did this one week, but a lion came and ate the second calf that he was trying to save. He and his son got the message and we do too: cooking something specifically for the Saturday night meal is desirable *and* adds even more honor to the mitzvah.

The food that the Children of Israel ate on Saturday nights during their forty years in the desert was the leftovers from the extra portion of manna that they received for Shabbat on Fridays. In the light of this, we can say that our Saturday night meal continues and completes the Shabbat meals and elevates them to an even more extraordinarily high level. [*Likutei Sichot,* vol. 36, p.75]

C. LUZ BONE

The Zohar tells us that every mitzvah has a corresponding part of the body, whether a limb or an organ or a vein, etc., and the fulfillment of any mitzvah nourishes the particular part of the body that corresponds to it. The Talmud declares that the part of the body nourished by the mitzvah-eating of the Saturday night meal is the *luz*. Most understand that it is the very small bone at the top of the spine.[1] [2]

The special quality of the *luz* is that it is the last part of the body to disintegrate in the grave, if indeed it ever does, and therefore it will be the starting place from which the body will

---

1 I have also heard it is the pituitary gland.

2 Rabbi **Yosef Caro**, one of the most important authorities on Jewish Law in the last thousand years, who lived in Tzefat in the 16th Century, refers to it as the "niskoi" bone (see *Beit Yosef* 300), the translation of which is unclear. it is also called simply "the resurrection bone."

be rebuilt at the Resurrection of the Dead,[3] when the time comes (see Talmud Sanhedrin 105a). So if you want to have a healthy resurrection, you know what to do on Saturday night!

It gets more interesting. Not only is the luz nourished from the food of Saturday night, it is nourished ONLY from the food on Saturday night. The Zohar points out that this means that unlike every other part of the body, it received no benefit from the eating of the fruit of the Tree of Knowledge. Therefore, the decree of death that descended upon mankind as a result of this sin did not and does not apply to the luz! That is why it is so resistant to decay, and merits to be the building block of the resurrection. And thus it can be said[4] that the inner dimension of the Saturday night meal is the rectification of that first sin of eating the forbidden fruit (before Shabbat arrived when it would have been permitted afterwards)!

d. NAMES OF THE MEAL

There are a number of names for this meal. The most popular is *Melaveh Malka*, which means escorting the Queen. Just as we welcome Queen Shabbat on Friday evening with candles, ceremony, and wine, so should we make a fuss over her with a celebratory meal when she departs, not just let her slip out the door.

Another name is The Fourth Meal. This emphasizes the continuity from Shabbat with its three meals. It is also known colloquially as King David's Meal, for reasons which I will soon set before you. These two latter names blend nicely together with a little stir-in from Kabbalah. On Shavuot, for the weekly reading from the Prophets, we read the first chapter of Ezekiel, which contains his vision of the Divine Chariot with the four different angels at its four sides. Corresponding to them, we are

---

3 The Hebrew word for bone, *'etsem'*, also means essence. The bones are the essential essence of the body. Therefore, only they are left at the end of the death process, and from them the body is to be rebuilt. (from an article by R. Peretz Auerbach on //KabbalaOnline.org)

4 The Lubavitcher Rebbe (*Likutei Sichot, Beshalach 5752*).

taught, are Abraham, Isaac, Jacob and David.

The Zohar adds that these four also correspond to the four meals. It turns out that King David's Meal is a shortened version of "סעודתא דדוד מלכא משיחא", (Seudata DeDavid Malka Meshicha) The Meal of David the Anointed King. The Zohar stresses that one should say at the meal, "דא היא סעודתא דדוד מלכא משיחא" —"*da he Seudata DeDavid Malka Meshicha*" (This is the Meal of David the Anointed King).

e. KING DAVID

It has even been said that King David originated the Saturday night meal as an occasion of joy. We know (see Talmud Shabbat 30a) that he cajoled the Al-mighty into revealing to him that the day of the week in which he would pass away would be Shabbat (Saturday). Which Shabbat, the date, was forbidden for him to know, he was told. So what did he do with this information? Every Shabbat, from beginning to end, he would study Torah (ibid. 30b), for the Angel of Death has no power over someone in the midst of focused Torah study (see Talmud Sota 21a — *Rashi*), because Torah is The Tree of Life. Even when he was eating, he would be thinking Torah thoughts. And it is said that if one falls asleep (if indeed King David slept on Shabbat) with a Torah thought and wakes with the same thought, it indicates then even when he was asleep he was engaged in Torah study! After Shabbat ended, on Saturday night, he would host a grand Thanksgiving meal, in gratitude that he was good to go for another week. Voila! — The Saturday Night Meal of King David.[5]

King David symbolizes *a*) the Jewish monarchy, *b*) Jerusalem

5 Actually, it didn't help him a bit when the appointed day came. At first the Angel of Death was confused about how to overcome him (Shabbat 30b), but then he quickly came up with a simple plan. He loudly rattled the fruit trees in the king's orchard behind the palace. David, still murmuring words of Torah, climbed the stairs to look out an upper window to see what was causing the disturbance. A step collapsed under him, and he was so startled that for a brief second he interrupted his recital ... and at that moment, which was of course the destined moment, he was taken.

(the city of David) and *c*) the Temple (the House of David), all of which express the idea of using Torah to make a dwelling place for G-d in the world. On Saturday night we channel the inspiration of Shabbat towards life-on-earth.[6]

f. KING MOSHIACH

Clearly, King David is the primary figure connected to the post-Shabbat meal. As part of that, in his role as the first "Anointed[7] King," he inspires us to pray for and act in a way that will invigorate the coming of his ultimate successor, *Melech HaMoshiach.*

For these reasons, it is understood that faithfully eating *Melaveh Malka* every week will hasten the coming of Moshiach.[8]

g. ELIJAH THE PROPHET

The title, The Meal of David the Anointed King, leads us to an expanded understanding of another wide-spread Saturday night custom, saying the name of *Eliyahu HaNavi* (Elijah the Prophet). The basic reason stated is that when he ascended to Heaven without dying first, he became an angel with the task of recording all the commandments that the Jews on earth successfully fulfill. Since we just finished fulfilling the mitzvah of Shabbat, one of the most important of all, we call on Elijah to make sure he writes us in the Heavenly record book.[9]

However, Elijah has another responsibility, as clearly stated in the Talmud. He is to be the advance man for King Moshiach. His

---

6 From ASCENT Quarterly #13 (Autumn 1988) — "How-To" Chart No. 6: *Melaveh Malka.*

7 The word in Hebrew for anointed is Moshiach. (That's right, the same title that is in the air so much these days.) It is an abbreviated one, short for Melech HaMoshiach — (The Messiah King). Only a king that is a direct descendant of David can be inaugurated by a prophet with the unique oil designated for this event. We pray at least three times a dayfor the Redeemer who will also be qualified to be the corner stone for the restoration of the Davidic dynasty.

8 *Likutei Sichot*, vol. 36, p.75

9 "Every Motzei Shabbat (Saturday night), Elijah enters Paradise, sits down under the Tree of Life, and records the merits of the Jews who keep Shabbat." — *Tosefta*

appearance several days before the actual revelation of Moshiach will signal us to intensify final preparations to welcome that world-changing event. So we petition him to come ASAP.[10]

Keeping all this in mind makes it difficult to be satisfied simply by pronouncing Eliyahu HaNavi just one time. Some repeat it different numbers of times. I've heard (or read[11]) 12,[12] 52,[13] 70, 100 & 130 times. However, many prefer to sing one or more of the popular Saturday night songs that weave his name into the lyrics multiple times.

Also, there is an old Sephardic custom to tell stories of Elijah on Saturday nights. (More on this in Section J below: Storytelling on Saturday night.)

h. MUSIC

Music is a beloved feature of Saturday night, as we ceased from it for the 25 hours of Shabbat. Playing musical instruments has traditional overlays too, because of the above-mentioned association of Saturday night with King David, the ultimate Jewish musician, the composer of the Psalms, which the world still lovingly recites 2,500 years later, and its accompanying music which has been lost to us since the destruction of the Holy Temples in Jerusalem. May we soon see the Third Temple in all its glory and holiness, and hear its unique music.

At Ascent-of-Safed on Saturday night, when the eating is mostly finished and the music has died down, and sometimes even before, the stories start. That's my job. I have been

---

10 "Prayers should be offered that he come speedily to bring us the tidings of redemption. Elijah will not come on Friday so as not to disturb Israel from preparing for Shabbat, nor do we pray for his coming on the Shabbat since he would not travel on it." — *Kitzur Shulchan Aruch*

11 In ASCENT Quarterly #13 (Autumn 1988) — "How-To" Chart No. 6: *Melaveh Malka* — see there for sources and also for more reasons than those here.

12 Because the last three letters of Eliyahu plus the first letter of HaNavi spell G-d's holy four-letter name, which has twelve permutations, each ascendant in a different month [and in a different hour of the day and of the night].

13 The numerical value of Eliyahu in Hebrew. The repetitions are said to help to have success in Torah study.

doing it most weeks for three decades, so now you know the laboratory where many of the stories you have read in this book were polished.

j. STORY-TELLING ON SATURDAY NIGHT

Story-telling about the great Jewish tzadikim (pure, righteous, spiritual giants) plays an important and beloved role on Saturday nights. How did that come about? Here comes another conjecture.

I mentioned above the long-standing custom of mentioning and invoking Elijah the Prophet on Saturday nights, for the reasons cited. Well, it is not a far journey from mentioning and invoking to telling stories about him, and indeed, doing so has long been a popular custom among Sephardic Jewry.

The chasidic movement exploded on the scene, and by the 1800's had spread all over the Jewish world, this included the custom of telling stories of the Baal Shem Tov on Saturday nights. The Sephardim also began to include telling stories about him and of course about many of their own many home-grown tzadikim as well. (A friend told me that when he was growing up in Mogador, Morocco, he thought the Baal Shem Tov also lived in Morocco somewhere!)

Once, a chasid of the *Be'er Mayim Chaim* (see story #16 in this book) visited the holy Rhizhiner Rebbe (see story #17 in this book), and heard from him, "Know that before the coming of *Mashiach*, faith and religion will be hanging by a thread. There will be great coldness in regard to faith. The way to survive spiritually will be for friends to gather on Shabbat or Motzei Shabbat and tell stories of tzadikim. That will help greatly in strengthening people's faith in G-d and in the tzadikim."

It is not my intention to say too much now about the importance of storytelling in general within Judaism. I am saving that topic for the Volume 3 appendix. Here I am restricting myself to its Saturday night role. Besides, if you got this far in this book, you must already have an appreciation of the helpfulness of stories about great Jewish personalities and our great G-d.

In conclusion, I'd like to leave you with a very short story about the importance of tzadikim/chasidic stories on Saturday nights, and three juicy quotes to further drive the point home.

— REBBETZIN RIVKAH* RELATED:

"One day in 5609 (1849 C.E.), when I was newly married, my father-in-law, the *Tzemach Tzedek* (the 3rd Rebbe of Chabad) called in all his daughters-in-law who lived in Lubavitch and instructed us to gather every Saturday night and tell a story of the Ba'al Shem Tov. We asked whether it was enough to just mention the Baal Shem Tov's name. My father-in-law replied, 'Definitely, a story!'

From that time on, one of the daughters-in-law would go into his room every Saturday night and he would tell her a story about the Baal Shem Tov. Afterwards the daughter-in-law would tell the story to the rest of us."

* The wife of the Rebbe Maharash, Rabbi Shmuel Schneersohn, the fourth Chabad Rebbe.

Source: *Lma'an Yishme'u* #112, based on *Sefer HaSichot 5700*, page 173

"We must believe all the stories, miracles, and wonders attributed to the Baal Shem Tov. We should believe that even if they didn't happen, they could have happened."

Rebbe Moshe of Kobrin (1784–1858 C.E.) as quoted in *Imros Tahoros*, p. 34

The ***Rhizhiner Rebbe*** used to teach:

"People say that relating a story of the Baal Shem Tov [founder of the chasidic movement] on Motzoei Shabbat [Saturday night] is helpful for parnassa [making a living] during the week. It is true, but it does not necessarily have to be about the Baal Shem Tov — it can be about any tzadik; and it is not only applicable on Saturday night — it can be anytime; and it helps not just for making a living — but for all matters of life."

The Torah discussions of the *Shabbat* table are theory; the *Melaveh Malka* story is a step toward practical application illustrating how the values of Judaism pervade actual life. As we tell the traditional stories of *Elijah the Prophet* roaming the world, the *Baal Shem Tov* spreading the light of G-d and dispelling the darkness of depression, the miracle-workings of great tzadikim, and/or the poignant pictures of the lives of simple, faithful Jews, we are in effect reminding ourselves that our lives during the coming week are also part of a great 'Story', the odyssey of the Divine Presence as we journey throughout the ages toward the ultimate goal of Redemption and Rectification.

Rabbi Moshe Y. Wisnefsky, in *Ascent Quarterly* #13 (Autumn 1988) — "How-To" Chart No. 6: *Melaveh Malka*

b. Some Laws, Customs, and Guidelines for the Saturday Night Meal

[Based primarily on ***Lma'an Yishme'u*** #86 (Parshat Vayakel 5771): "Accompanying the Queen," and ***The Ascent Complete Guide to Shabbat*** (ch. 7) by Rabbi Moshe Y. Wisnefsky (publication pending), as adapted by Yerachmiel Tilles for ***Ascent Quarterly*** #13 (Autumn 1988) — "How-To" Chart No. 6: ***Melaveh Malka***.]

1. When Shabbat leaves it is proper to accompany it, just as one accompanies royalty when they leave the city. Therefore, on Saturday night one should arrange a special meal, called *Melaveh Malka* (accompanying the Queen).

2. The special additional soul power granted to every Jew for Shabbat lingers until after Melaveh Malka.

3. It is preferable to wash hands and eat bread at Melaveh Malka.

4. One should set the table for a full meal, even if one will only eat a little bit, and even if one intends to eat only the minimum (one ounce) of food, which would entitle one to recite the appropriate thanksgiving blessing afterwards.

5. If one feels unable to eat bread, he can still fulfill this mitzvah by eating other foods.

6. It is appropriate to prepare a dish special for Melaveh Malka, not just eat Shabbat leftovers.

7. It is recommended to have a hot drink. Hot water on Saturday night is said to be soothing for depression, and helps one to be calm during the week.

8. This meal is considered a mitzvah occasion. Therefore, we light candles (without a blessing) at the table to enhance the festive mood.

9. Although the meal has the status of a mitzvah, there is no *kiddush* — Shabbat is over. Nor are there any obligatory prayers or verses to be said.

10. According to the Zohar, one should introduce the meal (in a manner parallel to the three Shabbat meals) by saying the Aramaic formula, "דא היא סעודתא דדוד מלכא משיחא" (This is the Meal of David, the Anointed King).

11. Eating the meal of Melaveh Malka with the orally expressed intention that the eating is in honor of the mitzvah of Melaveh Malka helps to ensure easy childbirth (Rebbe Elimelech of Lizhensk), and prolong one's life (the first Chortkover Rebbe).

12. It is customary to mention or sing about *Eliyahu HaNavi* (Elijah the Prophet). Some do this immediately after Havdalah; while others prefer to incorporate it into Melaveh Malka.

13. Storytelling about righteous Jewish personalities at Melaveh Malka is an important and popular custom.

14. Telling stories of Elijah the Prophet or the Baal Shem Tov on Saturday night is considered propitious for one's livelihood.

15. Some chasidic groups state that telling stories about the holy brothers, Rebbe Zushya and the Rebbe Elimelech (see story 11# in this book), is said to be an aid for those wishing to be blessed with children or to increase their fear of heaven (respectively).

16. Subsequent generations of rebbes declared that the stories can be about any great tzadik, and that it is beneficial for all of our material and spiritual needs.

17. It is best not to tend to other affairs until after Melaveh Malka.

18. A variety of opinions exist as to exactly when Melaveh Malka should take place on Saturday night: eat the meal as soon after Shabbat as possible; within four hours after Shabbat; or until midnight. It all depends on the season and your preference. Some start right after Havdala, while others delay until the house is straightened up, the kids put to bed, etc.

19. If one is prevented from making Melaveh Malka on Saturday night, it can be done on Sunday, or if impossible otherwise, even until Tuesday.

20. Even after Havdala on Saturday night, one should continue to wear Shabbos clothing. Some wear them until after Melaveh Malka, while others do not remove them until they go to sleep. Rebbe Yehoshua of Belz once said, "For however long one wears his Shabbos clothing on *Motzei Shabbos* (Saturday night), his stay in *Gan Eden* every Motzei Shabbos will be extended.

21. The holy Ari of Tzefat said that we should rejoice during the Saturday night meal as we do during the three meals of Shabbat.

22. Music is a popular (though not obligatory) element of Melaveh Malka. It may take the form of singing, listening to recordings as background, or attending a formal or informal live performance. The music should be of an

appropriate nature, Jewish religious music or at least music that contributes to the mood of the post-Shabbat occasion.

23. Many enjoy singing the special Saturday night songs at the table. One of the most popular is 'Do not fear, my servant Yaakov'. The Lubavitcher Rebbe once explained the significance of this song (even though it is not the Chabad custom to sing it): "After an entire day of not working, one may be afraid that he will be losing money, for his competition is open on Shabbos. G-d promises, 'Do not worry'. If you observe the commandments, He will provide for you as a master who must provide for a servant.

c. *Night of the Righteous*

By Meir Michel Abehsera

IT IS A PREVALENT CUSTOM among observant Jews to gather on Saturday night, singing and dancing and telling stories [sometimes even] until dawn. We extend the Shabbat that has technically passed, carrying some of its holiness with us into days of the week, the realm of the profane. It is the ideal time to speak about the righteous, the tzadikim. Any story or anecdote about them is a Shabbat in itself, a rest-stop for the Jew who is preparing to confront the weekdays. It is a place of transition where the mind is given ample time to ready itself for the mundane.

The spiritual forces of darkness have been starving during the entire length of the Shabbat. Therefore, you can only expect that as soon as Shabbat draws to its end, these forces will reach out to devour the defenseless. They lie in wait by the doors of every house of prayer and grab congregants by the dozen. One bite from the beast, and they are infused with an acute sense of the Saturday night blues.

Saturday night is a most sacred time, when exile is boxed in by redemption. It is a time when the nourishment of the spirit is most varied, when all duality is resolved. Intelligence is heightened, and everyone who celebrates the occasion is instantly wise. Doubts wane. Impossible questions are easily answered. The night exhausts itself, depositing a block of resolutions.

...Shabbat bathes the Jew in a bright and homogenous light which is not necessarily conducive to revelations of individual character. Shabbat is much too full, and therefore permits no contrast. Shabbat is the reservoir, not the conduit. It is contained within specific limits which allow no explosions to occur. Saturday night's light however, flickers relentlessly. It is a black fire whose pulsating luminescence disturbs and disperses the obtrusive layers that camouflage the soul. The Jew is never more conscious of his mission than during these hours. It is on this night that the world was created and on the very same night that light was made. Now, light is again renewed through our actions. As Shabbat draws to its end, and the obscurity of night begins to cover us with its black mantle, we burn a braided candle, whose variegated and animated flame rekindles the light of Creation.

Our holy masters say that the feeling of sadness we experience at Shabbat's end is caused by our subconscious sense of the primordial Shattering of the Vessels — that timeless, spaceless juncture in the history of Creation when the divine light fell into the lower worlds. We are given a taste of that decline. The light of Shabbat has flown back to its nest, and we search for it within. Some mystical writings compare that departure of the light to a deer fleeing from its pursuer, running with its head tilted under and to the side, staring back into your eyes. In that look of the deer, as the light recedes swiftly in the distance, we are given to retroactively appreciate the hidden reality of Shabbat.

It is said that at the beginning of Creation — meaning on Saturday night — [is when] the vessels prepared to hold the infinite light of Creation broke. On that same night, the repair of the vessels also began. Thus, we can only assume that there is no more opportune time to repair our own. Darkness was formed when work was left undone. The mundane week lies before us like an open abyss, auguring a reprise of that tragedy. The abyss beckons, and its pull is far out of proportion to our fragilities. The disparity is the main cause of Saturday night melancholia. The threat is real.

The threat is so real in fact, that one cannot possibly remain insensitive to it, since all of us descend from Adam, who was the first to experience the fall. It is said that upon seeing the sun set for the first time, he experienced a great anguish, certain that darkness had settled on the world because of his sin. That very same night, he took two stones and struck them one against the other until sparks flew. Though such a simple act seemed to hold little promise of transcendence, it was, in fact, the initial stroke that impelled him to return to the Garden of Eden. Poor though it may have been, the light of the fire gave him comfort, and so he blessed it. The memory of that past makes of Saturday night a most opportune time for new beginnings. Anticipation of something new happening is never so great, which is the reason why this night is known as the "Night of the Redeemer".

[For the full article, go to //www.kabbalaonline.org/kabbalah/article_cdo/aid/380589/jewish/Night-of-the-Righteous.htm, or better yet, buy Abehsera's book from which it was taken: "The Possible Man" (Swan House).]

—

Meir ("Michel") Abehsera was born in Morocco, and has lived there, Paris, Manhattan, Binghamton, Brooklyn, Los Angeles, Montreal, and now lives in Jerusalem. He is a pure Sephardi of distinguished ancestry (Abuchatzeira), and at the same time a devoted chasid of the Lubavitcher Rebbe. At various times he has been an engineer, a poet, a cook, a carpenter, a teacher, a best-selling author, a lecturer, and a healer.Every single one of the above elements plays its part in his highly original writing style, with tight intellectual organization of content and unusually elegant design, making The Possible Man, his magnus opus. More importantly, their integration with his penetrating honesty, his refined sense of playfulness, and, above all, his extraordinary love for his fellow beings, has enabled him to attract hundreds of wandering Jews to their roots. [Included among the latter are the author of this book and his wife.]

—

From *Ascent Quarterly* #30 (Spring 1994), p.6, as part of a review of *The Possible Man*.

Indices

a. Rabbis

b. Weekly Torah Readings

PARSHA	STORY #
Bereishis	–
Noach	17
Lech Lecha	9
Vayera	2, 4, 27
Chayei Sarah	–
Toldot	5
Vayetzei	7, 13
Vayishlach	–
Vayeishev	–
Miketz	28
Vayigash	8, 13
Vayechi	–
Shmot	7
Vaera	–
Bo	–
Beshalach	11
Yitro	9, 16
Mishpatim	18, 23, 24
Terumah	6
Tetzaveh	33
Ki Tisa	16
Vayakhel	5, 6
Pekudei	–
Vayikra	–
Tzav	–
Shemini	–
Tazria	9, 10
Metzorah	–
Acharei Mot	–
Kedoshim	24, 32
Emor	3
Bahar	18, 21, 29
Bechukotai	30
Bamidbar	–
Naso	–
Beha'alotecha	19
Shlach	–
Korach	–
Chukat	–
Balak	–
Pinchas	20
Matot	–
Massai	20
Devarim	–
Vaet'chanan	26
Ekev	22
Re'ei	18
Shoftim	12, 31
Ki Tetze	1
Ki Tavo	–
Netzavim	15, 25
Vayeilech	–
Haazinu	–
Zot Habracha	–

c. *Calendar Dates*

DATE		STORY #
Tishrei	2	27
	13	13, 22
	25	12
Cheshvan	3	17
	7	22
	11	10
Kislev	19	6
	27	16
Tevet	10	20, 26, 27
	24	13
Shvat	2	11
	10	28
	11	28
	23	23
Adar (pashut)	14	19
Adar-a	4	8
	18	32
	21	11
Adar-b	7	8
Nissan	2	25
	5	15
	11	30, 33
	13	2, 4, 18
	25	21
Iyar	1	9, 11
	2	22
	11	19
	20	10
Sivan	1	31
	2	24
	6	5, 7, 16, 19
Tammuz	3	30, 33
Menachem Av	5	1, 3
	9	14
Elul	18	5, 7

d. Themes & Topics

Dedicated in loving memory of
(Shaul) Paul Hegeman,
(a student in Ascent's very first program) by his parents,
Kathryn and Andrew Hegeman

Dedicated to the memory of my beloved sister,
Chana Rachel bat Sarah Dinah.
May her soul have an aliyah and bask in the glory of HaShem.
~ Jonathan Carp ~

In gratitude for the Shabbat night Tu B'Shvat Seder, 5773
at the home of Yerachmiel & Shulamit Tilles in Tsfat
Elliot and Duvie Goldofsky

To merit my four sons:

Yisroel Zev ben Raizel Sora,
Menachem Mendel ben Raizel Sora,
Tzvi Hirsh ben Raizel Sora,
Levi Yitzchak ben Raizel Sora

May the Al-mighty guide them to
find their good and proper soul mates very soon.

~ Raizel Sora Pershin ~

Dedicated in honor of

Malka-Ella bat Yehuda-Shmuel,
Chaya-Mushka bat Yehuda-Shmuel,
Yisrael-Aryeh-Leib ben Yehuda-Shmuel,
Golda-Hadassah bat Yehuda-Shmuel,
Michal bat Yosef-Yitzchak-Eliyahu

May they continue to give lots of nachas to their parents and grandparents,
and grow up to Torah, strong Jewish marriages, and multiple good deeds.

Author's Biography

Yerachmiel Tilles was born in 1945, in the Jewish month of Adar, which corresponds to the constellation and astrological sign of Pisces. In 1965, he graduated from Harpur College (SUNY Binghamton) with a Degree in Philosophy, accompanied by the dual distinctions of being president of the senior class and co-captain of Harper's basketball team.

For over two years, Tilles served as a Peace Corps volunteer teaching English in Thailand. In 1969, he was an overnight guest of the renowned author J.D. Salinger, and later owned and managed a macrobiotic restaurant. His life reached a turning point in 1971 when Tilles went to a synagogue for the first time in 13 years almost exactly from the day of his bar mitzvah. Within two years, Tilles had transformed into a Chasidic Jew and married. In early 1978, the author and his family moved to Israel, where they settled in Tzefat (Safed) a few months after their arrival and have lived there since.

In Tzefat, Tilles first taught English and was the managing partner of an art gallery. After that he studied Torah full-time for several years. In 1983, he co-founded the now legendary and very popular Ascent-of-Safed, and in 1984, he translated *A Mother in Israel* (Kehot Publications). Meanwhile, he and his wife were blessed with their first son in 1983, followed by a second son in 1988. These human blessings multiplied with the arrival of the first of their grandchildren in 2007.

In 1997, Tilles launched his weekly email distribution list for Chasidic stories, a weekly email that thousands of people eagerly await from week to week to this day. His next project was creating *KabbalaOnline.org* in 2001. The following year he became an 'answering scholar' on *AskMoses.com*.

From year to year, Tilles' repertoire of Chasidic stories has continued to grow and now numbers close to a thousand. Some stories found their way into small books of stories he wrote for his sons' weddings in 2006 and 2009. *Saturday Night, Full Moon*, the first of a three-volume series of Chasidic stories, was compiled in 2013. Volume 2, *Festivals of the Full Moon*, is slated for publication in 2014.